DOGS:
HOMOEOPATHIC REMEDIES

Other works by George Macleod

THE TREATMENT OF HORSES BY HOMOEOPATHY

THE TREATMENT OF CATTLE BY HOMOEOPATHY

A VETERINARY MATERIA MEDICA

CATS: HOMOEOPATHIC REMEDIES

GOATS: HOMOEOPATHIC REMEDIES

PIGS: THE HOMOEOPATHIC APPROACH TO THE TREATMENT
AND PREVENTION OF DISEASES

DOGS:
Homoeopathic Remedies

by

G. Macleod
MRCVS, DVSM, Vet. FF Hom

Index by
Francesca Garwood-Gowers

THE C. W. DANIEL CO. LTD.
SAFFRON WALDEN

First published in Great Britain by
the Homoeopathic Development Foundation Ltd

This edition was first published in 1989
by The C. W. Daniel Company Limited
1 Church Path, Saffron Walden
Essex, CB10 1JP, United Kingdom

ISBN 0 85207 218 X

Typeset by MS Typesetting, Castle Camps, Cambridge
and printed by Hillman Printers (Frome) Ltd, Frome, Somerset

Contents

Foreword

In this very brief foreword I would like to express my appreciation of the encouragement given to me by The Homoeopathic Development Foundation, who have co-operated with me and given guidance on various points. Also, I wish to express my thanks to Mrs. Diana Killick, who has typed the manuscript so expertly and who has persevered in the face of some rather unusual nomenclature.

Lindfield, November 1982   George Macleod

Preface

This outline of the commoner dog diseases and affections has been written in response to a growing demand on the part of homoeopathic owners and breeders for a text book which will provide a more detailed account of various conditions frequently encountered than those dealt with in the current handbook 'Homoeopathy for Pets'. No claim is made that it is exhaustive or complete in every detail and many remedies not listed may be needed for treatment depending on particular symptoms present in any one condition. However, the main ones have been noted. The potencies of remedies are a guide only and here again different ones may be needed. A good general guide is to use low potencies, e.g. 6 (centesimal) for the treatment of less acute conditions while reserving the higher potencies for those showing more acute symptoms. Repetition of the remedy is also a matter which will depend greatly on the response and progress of any affection. Acute conditions may need three or four doses in twenty-four hours while less acute ones could have the frequency reduced to twice weekly. Much will depend on the individual case and in this connection professional advice is always available.

Remedies should always if possible be given directly on the animal's tongue and are best employed as powders. The use of a small spoon will facilitate the operation. If tablets are employed, they should be enclosed in a small piece of bland food, e.g. wholemeal biscuit. Remedies should be stored in a cool, dry place away from direct sunlight and strong-smelling substances such as camphor, perfume, etc. The cap should never be left off the bottle.

The use of any mother tincture for external use requires a word of warning. Always see that such a tincture is diluted, especially for use on the eye as stinging or burning of the delicate mucous membranes could ensue if the neat tincture is used. One drop of mother tincture to one tablespoonful of water may be administered using an eye dropper.

Introduction

This book has been written in the hope that it will satisfy the needs of the many dog lovers who are interested in an alternative approach to the treatment of illnesses to which this endearing species is subject. It is by no means exhaustive and only the common remedies are listed in the text. For a detailed description of remedies the reader is referred to a more comprehensive manual of homoeopathic remedies.

Many of the non-specific conditions mentioned in the text are in many ways similar to those affecting the cat, but it has been found in practice that the response of the dog to any given remedy is different in many respects to that seen in the cat (or other species).

The general format of the text is on the same lines as that which obtains in the author's book on cats and the short materia medica of the commoner remedies is again the same.

WHAT IS HOMOEOPATHY?

For readers who have little or no knowledge of homoeopathic medicine a brief description of its essentials is necessary to the proper understanding of the role of the remedies in treatment.

Homoeopathy is a branch of medicine which states that any substance which can cause symptoms of illness in man or animal can also be used in the treatment of any condition showing similar symptoms. The principle of likeness between disease condition and remedy is emphasised. If we imagine the illness and the provings of the remedy representing two clinical pictures, we should endeavour as far as possible when treating to match one picture against the other. The closer the approximation of the two pictures (the likeness) the more likely we are to achieve satisfactory results in treatment. This is much easier to achieve in human than in veterinary medicine as subjective (mental) symptoms known only to the patient are difficult, if not impossible, to elicit in animals. Mental syptoms are extremely important in the treatment by homoeopathy of the human patient. Observation of an animal's behaviour and how it reacts to any given

1

situation, to other animals or people, to noise etc. will in some measure compensate for the lack of communication by speech. In certain circumstances it may be possible to imagine how the animal is feeling, e.g. the one which may feel grief at the loss of a companion, the one subjected to forced separation from the owner as in quarantine kennels, or those suffering post-operative psychological trauma.

Fortunately the homoeopathic materia medica contains remedies which are helpful in all these instances.

NATURE OF HOMOEOPATHIC REMEDIES

Homoeopathic remedies are obtained from all natural sources, e.g. plant and animal kingdoms and also minerals and their compounds with other chemicals. Homoeopathy is frequently referred to (quite erroneously) as herbal medicine. Nothing could be further from the truth as study of the previous remarks will show. While herbal medicine employs many plants successfully it is unable to exploit the intrinsic merits of plants in the way that homoeopathic medicine is able to do.

PREPARATION OF REMEDIES

Preparation of homoeopathic remedies is a scientific procedure which is best left to a qualified pharmacist trained in the particular techniques. Homoeopathy is too important for remedies to be prepared in any way but the best obtainable. Briefly, the system is based on a series of dilutions and succussions (of which more later) which is capable of rendering even a poisonous substance safe to use.

To prepare a potentised remedy, a measured drop of a solution called mother tincture (∅) derived from plant or biological material is added to 99 drops of a water/alcohol mixture and the resultant dilution subjected to a mechanical shock which is called succussion. This process which is essential to the preparation imparts energy to the medium which is rendered stable. One drop to 99 parts of water/alcohol mixture is represented by 1c on the centesimal scale. Preparations are also made on the decimal scale and marketed as 1x (on the continent as 1d). Repeated dilutions and successions yield higher potencies releasing more energy in the process. It will be appreciated therefore that homoeopathy is a system of medicine which concerns itself with energy and not with material doses of a drug.

After a dilution of 3c has been reached which represents 1/100,000 all poisonous or harmful effects of any substance are lost and only the curative properties remain.

SELECTION OF POTENCIES

Once the simillimum or 'most likely' remedy has been selected the question of which potency to use arises. As a general rule in the author's experience the higher potencies which are more energised than the lower should be employed in acute infections or conditions while the lower should be reserved for chronic conditions with or without pathological changes being present. It will be found occasionally that there are exceptions to this point of view and indeed many practitioners especially on the continent rely mostly on lower potencies for general use.

The potencies mentioned under each remedy in the text covering the various diseases are a guide only. Higher potencies than those mentioned will necessitate processional advice.

ADMINISTRATION OF REMEDIES

Remedies are marketed as medicated tablets and powders and also as tinctures and water dilutions. Owners must determine which system is the best for the particular animal being treated. Some dogs readily accept tablets, others powders and others again in liquid form by syringe. Extremely difficult animals can have the remedy incorporated in food or milk and while this is not ideal it has been shown in practice that remedies are equally effective if given in this way.

It is important to avoid subjecting the patient to undue stress and if the patient is unco-operative, the remedy should be given in food.

CARE OF REMEDIES

The delicate nature of the remedies which is inherent in their preparation renders them subject to contamination by strong-smelling substances, e.g. camphor, disinfectants etc. and also by strong sunlight. It is essential therefore that they be kept away from such influences and stored in a cool, dry place away from strong light. The use of amber glass bottles is helpful in this connection for storage of tablets.

NOSODES AND ORAL VACCINES

It will be noticed in the text under treatment of various specific conditions that reference is made to the term nosode, and it is necessary to explain fully to what this term refers.

A nosode (from the Greek NOSOS meaning disease) is a disease product obtained from any part of the system in a case of illness and thereafter potentised, e.g. canine distemper nosode prepared from various specimens of killed distemper exudate. In specific, i.e. bacterial, viral and protozoal, disease the causative organism may or may not be present in the material and the efficacy of the nosode in no way depends on the organism being present. The response of the tissues to invasion by bacteria or viruses results in the formation of substances which are in effect the basis of the nosode.

An oral vaccine is prepared from the actual organism which causes a disease and may derive from filtrates containing only the exotoxins of the bacteria or from emulsions containing both bacteria and their toxins. These filtrates and emulsions are then potentised and become oral vaccines.

There are two different ways of employing nosodes and oral vaccines:

1. Therapeutically and 2. Prophylactically

When we employ nosodes therapeutically we may use them for the condition from which the nosode was derived, e.g. canine distemper nosode in the treatment of distemper. This may be termed isopathic, i.e. treatment with a substance taken from an animal suffering from the same disease; or we may employ the nosode in any condition, the

4

symptoms of which resemble the symptom-complex of the particular nosode, e.g. the use of the nosode *Psorinum* in the treatment of the particular form of skin disease which appears in the provings of that nosode. This method may be termed homoeopathic, i.e. treatment with a substance taken from an animal suffering from a similar disease. In this connection it must be remembered that many nosodes have been proved in their own right, i.e. each has its own particular drug picture. Many veterinary nosodes have been developed but no provings exist for them and they are used almost entirely in the treatment or prevention of the associated diseases.

Autonosodes. This particular type of nosode is prepared from material provided by the patient alone, e.g. pus from a chronic sinus or fistula and after potentisation used for the treatment of the same patient. Many examples of this could be quoted but I think it is sufficient to explain the theory. Autonosodes are usually employed in refractory cases where well-indicated remedies have failed to produce the desired response and frequently they produce striking results.

Oral Vaccines. As with nosodes, oral vaccines may be used both therapeutically and prophylactically. If the condition is caused wholly by bacterial or viral invasion the use of the oral vaccine is frequently attended by spectacular success but this is less likely when there is an underlying chronic condition complicating an acute infection. Here we may need the help of constitutional and other remedies.

Bowel Nosodes. The bowel nosodes are usually included under the heading of oral vaccines as the potentised vaccines are prepared from cultures of the organisms themselves. As a preliminary introduction to the study of the bowel nosodes, let us consider the role of the E. coli organism. In the normal healthy animal the function of the E. coli bacteria is beneficial, rendering complex materials resulting from the digestive process into simpler substances. If however, the patient is subjected to any change, e.g. stress, which affects the intestinal mucosa, the balance between normal health and illness will be upset and the E. coli organisms may then be said to have become pathogenic. This change in the patient need not be a detrimental one, as the administration of potentised homoeopathic remedies can bring it about.

The illness therefore may originate in the patient which causes the bacteria to change their behaviour.

In laboratory tests it has been noticed that from a patient who had previously yielded only E. coli there suddenly appeared a large percentage of non-lactose fermenting bacilli of a type associated with the pathogenic group of typhoid and paratyphoid disease. Since the non-lactose fermenting bacilli had appeared after a latent period of 10–14 days following the administration of the remedy it would seem that the homoeopathic potentised remedy had changed the bowel flora. The pathogenic germ in this case was the result of vital stimulation set up in the patient by the potentised remedy; the germ was not the *cause* of any change. Each germ or bacillus is associated with its own peculiar symptom-picture and certain conclusions may be made from clinical and laboratory observation. These may be summarised as follows:

a) The specific organism is related to the disease.
b) The specific organism is related to the homoeopathic remedy.
c) The homoeopathic remedy is related to the disease.

The bowel nosodes which concern us in veterinary practice are as follows: 1. Morgan-Bach; 2. Proteus-Bach; 3. Gaertner-Bach; 4. Dys Co-Bach; 5. Sycotic Co-Paterson.

Morgan-Bach. Clinical observations have revealed the symptom-picture of the bacillus Morgan to cover in general digestive and respiratory systems with an action also on fibrous tissues and skin. It is used mainly in eczema of young dogs combined with an appropriate remedy, compatible ones being *SULPHUR*, *GRAPHITES*, *PETRO-LEUM* and *PSORINUM*.

Proteus-Bach. The central and peripheral nervous systems figure prominently in the provings of this nosode, e.g. convulsions and seizures together with spasm of the peripheral circulation; cramping of the muscles is a common feature; angio-neurotic oedema frequently occurs and there is marked sensitivity to ultra-violet light. Associated remedies are *CUPRUM METALLICUM* and *NATRUM MURIATICUM*.

Gaertner-Bach. Marked emaciation or malnutrition is associated with this nosode. Chronic gastro-enteritis occurs and there is a tendency for the animal to become infested with worms. There is an inability to digest fat. Associated remedies are *MERCURIUS, PHOSPHORUS* and *SILICEA*.

Dys Co-Bach. This nosode is chiefly concerned with the digestive and cardiac systems.

Pyloric spasms occurs with retention of digested stomach contents leading to vomiting. There is functional disturbance of the heart's action, sometimes seen in nervous dogs, usually associated with tension.

Associated remedies are *ARSENICUM ALBUM, ARGENTUM NITRICUM* and *KALMIA LATIFOLIA*.

Sycotic Co-Paterson. The keynote of this nosode is sub-acute or chronic inflammation of mucous membranes especially those of the intestinal tract where a chronic catarrhal enteritis occurs. Chronic bronchitis and nasal catarrh are met with.

Associated remedies are *MERCURIUS CORROSIVUS, NITRICUM ACIDUM* and *HYDRASTIS*.

MAIN INDICATIONS FOR THE USE OF THE BOWEL NOSODES

When a case is presented showing one or two leading symptoms which suggest a particular remedy we should employ that remedy, if necessary in varying potencies, before abandoning it and resorting to another if unsatisfactory results ensue. In chronic disease there may be conflicting symptoms which suggest several competing remedies and it is here that the bowel nosodes may be used with advantage. A study of the associated remedies will usually lead us to the particular nosode to be employed. The question of potency and repetition of dosage assumes special importance when considering the use of bowel nosodes. The mental and emotional symptoms which frequently present in illness in the human being are not available to a veterinary surgeon and he therefore concerns himself with objective signs and pathological change. The low to medium potencies, e.g. 6c–30c are more suitable for this purpose than the higher ones and can be safely administered daily for a few days. Bowel nosodes are deep-acting remedies and should not be repeated until a few months have elapsed since the first prescription.

I acknowledge the pamphlet written by the late Dr. John Paterson.

Vaccination Procedure

This is based on the use of nosodes and/or oral vaccines. There is no hard and fast rule concerning frequency of administration but a system which has yielded satisfactory results is to give a single dose (powder or tablet) night and morning for 3 days followed by one per week for 4 weeks and continuing thereafter with a monthly dose for 6 months.

There is a fundamental difference between conventional vaccination by injection and that using the oral route. The former involves the subcutaneous or intramuscular injection of an antigen (vaccine material) which after an interval produces antibodies in the bloodstream against the particular antigen. While in most cases by this method a degree of protection against the particular disease is established, the procedure can be criticised on two grounds: 1, The defence system of the body is not fully incorporated by this means and 2, there is a risk of side effects due to the foreign nature of the protein involved in the vaccine material. This aspect of conventional vaccination has been well-documented in many species.

Oral vaccination on the other hand gives a more solid immunity inasmuch as it incorporates the entire defence system, which is mobilised as soon as the vaccine is taken into the mouth and builds up protection with each further dose. This build-up leads on from tonsillar tissue through the lymphatics incorporating the entire reticulo-endothelial system. This procedure is equivalent to what is known as 'street infection' viz. ingestion of virus etc. during daily contact with other animals, when immunity would be built up in the same way.

Another advantage in protection by homoeopathic means is that vaccination can be started very early in the puppy's life, e.g. within the first week if necessary. This does not interfere with the presence of any maternal antibodies.

Footnote. The undesirable side-effects which sometimes follow conventional vaccination can in some measure be offset by the use of the potentised virus using ascending potencies at varying intervals depending on the severity of the case.

VACCINATION PROCEDURE

There are no side effects when using homoeopathic oral vaccines – a reaction may sometimes be observed, as also occasionally with remedies but such reaction is transient and soon passes.

Diseases of the Digestive System

These diseases are extremely common in dogs and range from conditions affecting the mouth down to the lower end of the alimentary canal. It is convenient to subdivide these diseases according to the organ or organs concerned, viz:

1. Lips and Mouth
2. Mouth, involving teeth, gums, tongue and salivary glands
3. Pharynx and Oesophagus
4. Stomach
5. Small and large intestines including rectum
6. Liver and Pancreas

1. LIPS

Inflammation of Lips. This may take several forms and be due to many factors, chief among which are mechanical injuries including damage by excessive tartar on canine teeth and ulceration which may extend to the commissures of the lips. It may also be due to infection, e.g. Staphylococcal producing a dermatitis which may progress to abscess formation.

CLINICAL SIGNS The animal will probably be noticed pawing at the mouth and the lips may show swelling. The surrounding areas are sometimes stained brown. Salivation is invariably present accompanying ulceration of varying degree. Loss of hair on surrounding areas is frequently seen.

TREATMENT
1. ACID NIT. 30c. This is one of the chief remedies for treatment of ulcerated surfaces near the body orifices. There may be an accompanying corneal ulceration together with salivation and bleeding gums. The ulcerated surfaces usually discharge offensive material.

2. MERC. CORR. 30c. When this remedy is indicated, the mouth is usually very offensive with profuse slimy salivation and bleeding gums. Frequently there is blood-stained nasal discharge while slimy diarrhoea with tenesmus may arise.

3. RHUS TOX. 6c. Indicated when the inflammation is manifested by deep red discoloration and papules which develop into vesicles and ulcers. Itching is usually severe. The inflammatory process extends into the mouth giving bright red gums, tongue and throat.

4. HEPAR SULPH. 30c. This remedy may be needed when abscesses develop which are extremely sensitive to touch. The animal resents contact and will refuse food. High potencies of this remedy will help abort the suppurative process while low ones may hasten discharge of purulent material.

5. CALC. SULPH. 6x. Once abscesses have matured and are discharging, this remedy will be of use. It should be reserved for those cases where pus has actually found an outlet.

6. BORAX 6c. When the ulcers on the lips extend into the mouth and produce raw aphthous ulcerated surfaces where the epithelium is easily peeled off. Salivation is profuse. Vomiting may occur along with a mucous diarrhoea.

7. STAPHYLOCOCCUS NOSODE 30c. If abscesses arise which are suspected to be bacterial in origin, the use of this nosode will help as Staphylococci are the main bacteria involved.

2 (a) STOMATITIS – Inflammation of mouth
GINGIVITIS – Inflammation of gums

Stomatitis is the general term used to cover any inflammatory process affecting the mouth generally, while Gingivitis refers specifically to the gums. Sometimes the term 'Glossitis' is used if the tongue alone is inflamed.

ETIOLOGY. Stomatitis and gingivitis may be the result of any localised inflammatory process or be due to an extension of the process from the gums, or to mechanical changes. Non-specific causes include Vitamin B1 deficiency and kidney failure bringing on a threatened Uraemia. Main causes are Vincents stomatitis and the Distemper/ Hepatitis/Leptospirosis complex.

CLINICAL SIGNS. Salivation is usually present and the appetite is in abeyance. Food is chewed very carefully. Redness of mucous membranes is apparent and in severe cases ulceration occurs. Gingivitis produces bleeding of gums and ulceration of the peridontal areas, which become swollen and tender. Necrotic lesions on tongue and pharynx appear in very severe outbreaks. If stomatitis is due to a uraemic syndrome, the mucous membranes become dark and there is a pronounced urinary smell from the mouth.

TREATMENT. There are a number of useful remedies for consideration and it may be necessary to watch carefully for accompanying systemic symptoms before deciding on any particular one.

1. BAPTISIA 30c. Salivation accompanying offensive breath and yellowish-brown discoloration of tongue and gums may signify the need for this remedy. Tonsils and throat become dark red, the inflammation making swallowing difficult. Vomiting may occur with other alimentary complications such as dysenteric stools. Prostration is frequently present and the animal may give an impression of generalised toxaemia.

2. ACID. MURIATICUM 30c. Ulceration of lips occurs with swelling of neighbouring lymphatic glands. Gums become swollen and the throat is darkened and oedematous. When urine is passed there may be an accompanying passage of faeces.

3. ACID. NIT. 30c. This remedy is especially suitable for ulceration of those parts which are nearest the lips. Salivation is again a feature and coalescence of ulcers may occur. Gums bleed easily when this remedy is indicated.

4. BORAX 6c. Indications for this remedy are an aphthous appearance of the ulcers and the fact that the epithelium peels easily. Salivation is frothy and takes the form of long drooling strands. There may be involvement of the inter-digital spaces where vesicles may form.

5. ACID. FLUOR. 30c. Dental fistulae are common when this remedy is indicated. Saliva becomes blood-stained. The teeth may show evidence of necrosis. Throat ulceration accompanies a desire for cold water. Warm drinks may bring on bouts of diarrhoea. The necrotic process may extend to the bones of the upper jaw.

6. *MERC. CORR. 30c.* Slimy, blood-stained salivation is present when this remedy is needed. The whole mouth is extremely offensive and dirty with involvement of all structures. Teeth appear dingy and swelling of throat and neighbouring lymph glands takes place. Systemic complications include dysenteric slimy stools and possibly greenish nasal discharges.

7. *KREOSOTUM 30c.* One of the keynotes of this remedy is rapid decay of teeth on eruption and accompanying a spongy condition of bleeding gums, which show a tendency to gangrene. Vomiting of blood may occur, together with diarrhoea of blackish putrid material. It could also be useful in those cases associated with uraemic tendencies.

8. *CARBOLIC ACID 30c.* The throat is chiefly affected when this remedy is indicated, diphtheritic lesions appearing. Dark green vomition occurs with flatulence and blood-stained diarrhoea following severe enteritis. The urine assumes a dark green colour.

9. *RHUS TOX. 1M.* Dark red inflammation with papules and later vesicles signifies this remedy. The throat is again involved showing dark red inflammatory patches. Systemic symptoms include vesicular inflammation of the skin with severe itching.

10. *ACID. SULPH. 30c.* Gums bleed easily, leaving a bruised dark red look. The blood is dark or black. Eye symptoms such as redness of the conjunctiva and small haemorrhages are frequently present when this remedy is indicated.

2 (b) ALVEOLAR PERIOSTITIS. PERIODONTITIS

This condition is associated with the build-up and accumulation of tartar on the teeth. This provides a suitable base for the proliferation of bacteria which then invade the alveolus resulting in its destruction. This in turn causes loosening of the tooth. Gingivitis is a more or less constant accompaniment. The longer the condition persists, the more likely it is for pyogenic bacteria to produce abscesses in the alveolus.

Extensive disease may cause destruction of surrounding bone with the threat of osteomyelitis developing.

TREATMENT. All tartar should be removed and the teeth properly cleaned. Removal of tartar should be undertaken every 4-6 months, and a diet containing adequate meat with the minimum of carbohydrates will help reduce its formation. The following remedies will help:

1. *MERC. CORR. 30c.* This is primarily for the gingivitis associated with the condition and will be of use even after abscess formation has taken place.

2. *ACID. FLUOR. 30c.* If the disease has progressed to include the facial bones, this remedy will help allay the tendency to necrosis.

3. *SILICEA 30c.* This remedy is of use when suppuration of the alveolus occurs with threatened osteomyelitis of surrounding bone.

4. *FRAGARIA 6c.* A remedy which will help prevent excessive deposition of tartar and should be given at regular intervals to dogs after they have reached two years old.

2 (c) EPULIS

This is the name given to a fibrous tumour which develops on the gum. It is benign and has its origin in some chronic inflammatory process. It frequently contains bony material. It may appear singly or in clumps, and is commonest in brachycephalic breeds.

TREATMENT. They are usually treated by excision with electrocautery. If this is unacceptable, the following remedies should provide a suitable alternative:

1. *HECLA LAVA 30c.* This is a most useful remedy for the treatment of bony tumours affecting the upper jaw especially. It may be necessary to proceed through rising potencies to achieve best results.

2. *CALC. FLUOR. 30c.* Indicated more for the more fibrous and less bony tumour. This is a deep-acting remedy and should not be repeated too frequently. One dose per week for two months should suffice.

3. *CALC. CARB. 30c.* A useful remedy for the fat or obese animal, especially young subjects. There may be a generalised skeletal weakness when this remedy is needed.

4. SILICEA 30c. Has some reputation in the treatment of bony tumours and might be considered if *HECLA* fails to produce satisfactory results.

2 (d) GLOSSITIS

Inflammation of the tongue may be primary due to mechanical injury or secondary when it results as a sequel to some systemic disease. A form of gangrenous glossitis may follow ingestion by leptospiral organisms or be associated with chronic nephritis.

CLINICAL SIGNS. Loss of appetite and putrid breath accompany salivation of varying degrees. In the gangrenous type a tough exudate forms on the top of the tongue. This rapidly becomes necrotic, the colour changing from dark-red to grey. Severe pain is present. If the disease is unchecked, sloughing of the tip of the tongue takes place.

TREATMENT
The following remedies should be considered:

1. KREOSOTUM 30c. This is a useful remedy for gangrenous tendencies of the oral cavity in general. It could be useful in the early stages when dark red discoloration is evident. A further indication for its use would be toxaemic complications which frequently accompany the condition.

2. SECALE 30c. A most valuable remedy when threatened gangrene is evident due to restriction of blood supply to the tip of the tongue. It could be of use even at the stage of greyish discoloration indicating necrosis, and should enable blood supply to be restored normally.

3. MERC. CORR. 30c. If the condition is associated with chronic nephritis, this remedy will help by treating the basic condition as it is a main remedy in dealing with kidney disease. By itself it will help remove the foul smell and salivation.

4. PHOSPHORUS 30c. This remedy is also associated with a basic nephritis, and when it is indicated there are usually accompanying small haemorrhages on the gums. Systemic complications include vomiting when food or water becomes warm in the stomach.

5. LEPTOSPIROSIS NOSODE 30c. This nosode should always be used in conjunction with other indicated remedies if it is considered that Leptospirosis has been contracted. A single dose should suffice.

2 (e) THE SALIVARY GLANDS

These glands concern us because of their role in the production of saliva. They may become the seat of infection or cysts may develop in one or other of them. Overproduction of saliva is called Ptyalism and may arise as a result of car sickness or stomatitis due to various causes. Signs are obvious and the excess of saliva if swallowed may result in vomiting. The main remedies to be considered in Ptyalism are as follows:—

1. PILOCARPUS 30c. The submaxillary and parotid glands become swollen when this remedy is indicated and there may be profuse diarrhoea with straining.

2. ACONITUM 6c. If attacks come on suddenly and are associated with temperature rise, Aconite will prove useful.

3. MERC. SOL. 6c. If stomatitis is the cause, this remedy will be of use and help reduce the output of saliva by removing the basic inflammation.

4. BORAX 6c. When this remedy is indicated saliva takes the form of frothy strands with vesicles on gums and tongue.

Infection of the glands may result in abscesses producing firm and painful swelling of the structure accompanied by systemic changes and a rise in temperature. The animal is unwilling to open the mouth. Oedema may be seen around the base of the ear if the parotid gland is involved.

TREATMENT OF INFECTED GLANDS

1. PHYTOLACCA 30c. Glandular swellings are a keynote of this remedy. The glands are firm and swollen and dark-red discoloration of the throat takes place. Tonsillar tissue becomes swollen, making swallowing difficult.

2. ACONITUM 6c. If temperature rises and attacks come on suddenly or as a result of exposure to cold dry winds, this remedy will help.

3. APIS MEL. 30c. When oedema develops around the base of the ear from an extension of parotid gland inflammation, Apis will be found useful.

4. MERC. IOD. RUB. 9c. The red iodide of mercury has a good reputation for reducing inflammation of glands on the left side of the throat region. The submaxillary glands are less affected.

5. MERC. IOD. FLAV. 9c. The yellow iodide of mercury has a similar action but has reference mainly to the right side of throat and throat glands.

6. HEPAR SULPH. 30c. This potency of Hepar will help allay the suppurative process if glands become infected, especially if they are extremely sensitive to touch.

7. SILICEA 30c. More chronic forms of suppuration will be catered for by this remedy. Pus tends to become inspissated and the glands remain hard. If cysts develop in the salivary glands, the resulting fluid may be controlled by *APIS 30c.* followed by a course of *IODUM 30c.* if surgical interference is ruled out.

3 DISEASES OF PHARYNX AND OESOPHAGUS

a) PHARYNGITIS. Inflammation of the pharynx may arise as a direct result of injury from some traumatic agent but more usually the trouble is secondary to some constitutional disease such as the Distemper/Hepatitis/Leptospirosis complex. Extension of local infection also takes place and in these cases species of Streptococci and Staphylococci are involved.

CLINICAL SIGNS. There is a primary temperature rise and the dog may be off its food. Hawking of white foamy mucus occurs. Severe cases show involvement of neighbouring lymph glands and excess production of saliva is also seen. On examination the throat appears dark-red and there may be membranous deposits and ulcerations present.

TREATMENT. There are many useful remedies available, chief among which are the following:

1. ACONITUM 6c. Should always be given in the early stages when rise of temperature occurs. The early use of this remedy frequently obviates the need for anything else.

2. FERRUM PHOS. 6. This is also a very useful remedy for the early stages. It differs from *ACONITUM* in showing ulceration with a generalised redness of the mouth. Extension of the inflammatory process frequently involves the ears, and the pulse is usually soft in contrast to that obtaining when *ACONITUM* is indicated. Generally it is to be preferred for the less severe case.

3. BELLADONNA 30c. With this remedy the papillae of the mouth show swelling and the throat is red and puffy-looking. Accompanying signs include dilation of pupils with a full bounding pulse, and an overall feeling of heat.

4. MERC. CYANATUS 30c. This is one of the most important remedies for pharyngitis showing the presence of a diphtheritic membrane of greyish colour which peels off leaving a necrotic area. Neighbouring salivary glands are swollen and tender. There may be accompanying vomiting of blood-stained bile.

5. PHYTOLACCA 30c. Throat involvement takes the form of dark-red discoloration with swelling of tonsillar tissue. The parotid salivary glands in particular become swollen and tender. There may be generalised glandular swelling, with accompanying prostration when this remedy is indicated.

6. MERC. IOD. RUB. 9c. The throat is involved more on the left side and there is an associated stiffness of neck muscles. The salivary glands on the left side are usually the seat of inflammation before the throat shows lesions.

7. MERC. IOD. FLAV. 9c. The indications for this remedy are the same as for the preceding one with the difference that the right hand areas are involved.

8. RHUS TOX. 1M. Dark-red diffuse discoloration of mouth and throat with watering of eyes may indicate this remedy. Signs of orbital cellulitis may be present, along with thirst and a mucous dysentery.

9. APIS MEL. 30c. If there is pronounced oedema present impeding breathing, the use of this remedy will hasten its absorption. The throat appears swollen and is puffy on palpation. The tongue also may be swollen and stools are brownish and watery. The condition may be associated with an incipient nephritis.

FOOTNOTE. If pharyngitis is thought to be a sequel to infection by Distemper, Hepatitis or Leptospirosis the use of the appropriate nosode will be indicated along with indicated remedies. Streptococcus and Staphylococcus nosodes may also be employed this way if it is thought that bacteria of these species are implicated.

3 (b) OESOPHAGITIS Inflammation of the oesophagus is usually secondary to some mechanical injury, e.g. the presence of some foreign body.

CLINICAL SIGNS. Lack of appetite usually brings to the notice of the owner that all is not well. If food is taken where appetite is not wholly lost it soon becomes regurgitated. Salivation is usually profuse. The dog makes repeated attempts to swallow even when food is not present.

TREATMENT. The following remedies may give relief and help soothe the oesophageal lining:

1.   MERC. CORR. 30c. Has a reputation for soothing inflammatory or ulcerated mucous membranes. Especially indicated when excess saliva is present.

2.   PHOSPHORUS 30c. This remedy is associated with an extension of the inflammatory process to the stomach, causing vomiting at frequent intervals.

3.   ACID. SULPH. 30c. This remedy is generally associated with healing of mucous membranes injured by foreign bodies or showing threatened gangrene. Saliva is probably blood-stained when this remedy is indicated.

4.   CARBO VEG. 200c. The dog shows extreme tenderness over the epigastric region and there may be aphthous-looking ulcers in the mouth.

4   THE STOMACH

a)   GASTRITIS (ACUTE). Inflammation of the stomach is extremely common and is usually due to irritant factors of one kind or another. It can also arise as a sequel or accompaniment to acute infectious diseases such as Hepatitis and Leptospirosis.

CLINICAL SIGNS. There is invariably constant thirst and vomiting, with a temperature rise if the condition is associated with infectious disease. Pain on palpation of the stomach region is usually present. Signs of dehydration quickly set in especially if vomiting is severe or prolonged and is worse in puppies and young animals.

TREATMENT. There are a considerable number of remedies available for the control of vomiting and it is impossible to list them all. Reference would need to be made to a standard Materia Medica to determine which one would fit the individual animal. However, the following remedies will probably help the average case:

1. *PHOSPHORUS 30c.* With this remedy there is pronounced thirst but vomiting takes place as soon as the contents of the stomach become warm after drinking (or eating). The gums may be ulcerated and show small haemorrhages. Stools may be clay-coloured.

2. *MERC. CORR. 30c.* Vomiting may take the form of greenish bile-stained mucus possibly with flecks of blood. There may be an accompanying dysentery with foul mouth and profuse salivation.

3. *IPECACUANHA 30c.* Retching and vomiting may lead to collapse. The vomit is slimy and may be continuous. Slimy diarrhoea, possibly blood-stained, may also be present. There may also be reflex respiratory symptoms such as coughing and difficult breathing.

4. *ANTIMONIUM TART. 30c.* The tongue is coated, with red edges. Swallowing is difficult and accompanied by retching and vomiting. Rumbling of intestines may be heard preceding stool which is accompanied by straining, the stools themselves being watery with shreds of mucus.

5. *ARSEN. ALB. 30c.* When this remedy is indicated, the mouth is ulcerated and dry. Thirst is prominent but there is desire for small quantities only. The contents of the vomitus are blood-stained or may contain whole full blood. The animal is usually restless, changing position frequently and all symptoms become worse toward and after midnight. The coat is dry and harsh as a rule.

6. *IODUM 30c.* This remedy may be suitable for the lean animal showing cadaverous hunger with diarrhoea of a pale frothy character.

Mouth and tongue may show aphthous ulcers. Liver complications are a common feature with signs of jaundice in visible mucous membranes.

7. *AETHUSA 6c.* Aphthous lesions are also associated with this remedy and in addition there are pustular eruptions on the throat. There is a marked intolerance of milk which is vomited in curd form. Frothy white vomition occurs shortly after ingestion of food. The stool is undigested, greenish and thin. Young suckling animals will benefit from this remedy, such subjects showing also a tendency to collapse with cholera-like symptoms.

8. *IRIS VERS. 30c.* Vomition of biliary material accompanies colic and diarrhoea with tenderness over the liver region. Signs of jaundice may appear. It is a useful remedy if gastritis and vomiting are thought to arise from liver or pancreatic dysfunction.

9. *PETROLEUM 6c.* Vomitus is sour-smelling and water accumulates readily in the mouth when this remedy is indicated. Passage of stool is followed by hunger which relieves temporarily. Diarrhoea is watery and confined to daylight hours.

10. *APOMORPHINE 6c.* This remedy may be needed for sudden and reflex vomiting. Mucous salivation is usually present. The animal feels hot with dilated pupils.

11. *NUX VOM. 6c.* Stools are generally hard when this remedy is needed. Gastritis is usually due to overeating, especially of rich or unsuitable food.

b) **CHRONIC GASTRITIS.** This is usually the result of constant irritation due to some foreign body and takes the form of intermittent vomiting which can take place independently of eating or drinking. Such animals show inappetance and progressive loss of weight with harsh staring coats. Signs of anaemia are evidence in severe cases. The principal remedies to consider are *PHOSPHORUS* 30c. indicated for the animal which shows flecks of blood in the vomit and is worse after eating. *ARSEN. ALB.* 30c. is useful for restoring condition to the coat and reducing the tendency to anaemia. Ascending potencies of *ARSEN. ALB.* may be needed to establish a long-term cure in such cases. Frequently the condition is related to an underlying chronic kidney upset and remedies to deal with this will be included in the section on kidney diseases.

5 DISEASES OF SMALL AND LARGE INTESTINES

a) PYLORIC STENOSIS. This may be congenital or acquired and in the latter it is usually secondary to some chronic inflammatory process which produces scar tissue and consequent narrowing of the pylorus.

CLINICAL SIGNS. Severe vomiting is the rule, while appetite is maintained. The vomiting is independent of food or water and may arise after a few hours of food intake. Constipation is usually present.

TREATMENT. If surgery is not contemplated the following remedies may help:

1. *NUX VOM. 1M.* Vomiting may be accompanied by severe retching. The stomach region is sensitive to touch.
2. *LYCOPODIUM 1M.* Digestion is generally weak. More adapted to lean animals or thin breeds of dogs. Very little food satisfies. General abdominal flatulence is present.
3. *SILICEA 30c.* This is a very useful remedy for reducing scar tissue and may help indirectly by acting on the chronic inflammatory process in this way.

b) ENTERO-COLITIS. Inflammation of intestines. It is convenient to include under this heading both large and small intestines. Conditions affecting the latter are more common than those which involve the small gut. Inflammatory condition of the intestines results in diarrhoea and/or dysentery, the character of the stool varying considerably.

a) **ACUTE ENTERO-COLITIS.** This may arise as a result of bacterial attack including specific diseases such as Distemper, Leptospirosis etc. and also through faulty feeding, e.g. ingestion of decomposing foodstuffs.

CLINICAL SIGNS. Vomiting may be seen initially but the main symptom is diarrhoea which may at times be haemorrhagic. Temperature may rise if the attack is due to bacterial invasion but if poisoning is suspected the temperature is usually sub-normal. Pain is evident on abdominal palpation and rumbling of gut may be heard in the large bowel. Signs of dehydration appear if the diarrhoea is prolonged.

TREATMENT. The homoeopathic practitioner is fortunate in having a wide range of remedies available for treatment of this condition according to the detailed symptoms involved. The following represent just a few of the many which may be indicated. It is not possible to list them all and reference may need to be made to a standard Materia Medica to find a specific remedy.

1. ARSEN. ALB. 6c or 30c. This remedy is associated with watery stools of a cadaverous odour, frequently worse in the evening or towards midnight. Thirst for small amounts of water is usual. The coat is harsh and dry and the patient is restless, changing position from time to time. This is a good remedy to employ in the animal which is showing signs of dehydration.

2. IPECAC. 30c. Indicated when severe vomiting precedes an attack. Frequent mucoid stools which are greenish in colour and may also be tinged with blood.

3. ALOE 200c. Stools are lumpy and jelly-like and frequently passed involuntarily. There may be an underlying liver congestion present. Flatulence is heard in the large bowel as rumbling.

4. PODOPHYLLUM 30c. This is a frequently-indicated remedy for conditions affecting both small and large intestines resulting in a gushing type of watery stool which may contain mucus. It is suitable for diarrhoea of long-standing and may be accompanied by a degree of rectal prolapse.

5. MERC. CORR. 30c. A most important remedy for the dysenteric stool which contains mucus and has a slimy appearance. Symptoms become worse in the period from sunset to sunrise. Severe straining accompanies passage of the stool.

6. VERATRUM ALB. 30c. Prostration accompanies the diarrhoea and there is a general picture of collapse. Signs of colic precede the onset of diarrhoea which is profuse and watery. General signs include dry mouth and cyanosis of visible mucous membranes.

7. CAMPHORA 6c. Prostration is again evident with this remedy but the picture is more severe than with VERATRUM ALB. The entire body becomes cold while the stool itself is blackish and passed involuntarily.

8. CUPRUM MET. 30c. Muscular cramping may be seen accompanying diarrhoea of a greenish, blood-stained character. Nervous symptoms are often present, e.g. twitchings.

9. CARBO VEG. 200c. A most useful remedy for the moribund animal and will frequently give dramatic results in apparently hopeless cases which have suffered severe fluid loss. The stools have a cadaverous odour and are attended by considerable flatus.

10. PYROGEN 1M. This is another remedy frequently indicated for the extreme case. Stools are generally putrid and there is often a state of gross toxaemia. A guide to the use of the remedy is a high temperature alternating with a weak, thready pulse.

11. CHINA 6c. This remedy should always be given as an accompaniment to others as it will help restore strength after loss of body-fluid. By itself it may control the diarrhoea.

12. ACONITUM 6c. Although not generally used as a remedy for diarrhoea as such, this remedy should be given as soon as symptoms of illness arise, especially in the case of specific disease.

b) **CHRONIC ENTERO-COLITIS.** The main symptom attending this condition is a chronic diarrhoea which may have its origin in the presence of foreign bodies or worms. The effects of tumour formation and pancreatic or liver disease may also contribute to it. Other causes include kidney disease and nervous upsets.

CLINICAL SIGNS. On abdominal palpation it may be possible to feel a thickening of the lower bowel. Stools become mucoid and from time to time are streaked with blood. There is a progressive loss of condition accompanying dehydration.

TREATMENT. The remedies outlined for the acute condition are again applicable to the chronic form, since diarrhoea of one kind or another is the chief symptom present. The addition of *SILICEA 30c.* should have a beneficial effect on the thickened bowel.

c) **ULCERATIVE COLITIS.** This particular form of colitis is usually confined to young animals, especially those up to two years old. The Boxer breed is particularly susceptible.

CLINICAL SIGNS. The general condition of the animal remains good and the only important sign is the passage of soft stools containing a preponderance of mucus and showing streaks of blood. The character of the stool varies and is passed frequently, the colour being a lightish brown.

TREATMENT. Many of the remedies mentioned under Entero-colitis will again be applicable depending on the type of diarrhoea present. In addition the following remedies are more specifically indicated:

1.   ACID. NIT. 200c. This is a remedy which is particularly suitable when ulceration of mucous membranes occurs near the outlet of natural orifices, and will therefore be indicated for those cases which develop lesions in the rectum as an extension from the colon.

2.   MERC. DULC. 30c. This remedy has proved useful in mild cases which show occasional mucoid stools with possible mouth ulceration. Stools are scanty although passed more often than usual.

3.   KALI BICH. 200c. A suitable remedy when the stools become jelly-like and are passed more frequently in the mornings. Severe straining may accompany the passage of the stool and dysentery is often present.

4.   IODUM 6c. When stools become frothy and yellow and are accompanied by voracious appetite and loss of condition. The skin has a dehydrated look.

5.   CHAMOMILLA 6c. This is a useful remedy for controlling diarrhoea associated with upsets in the young animal. Stools are hot and slimy and excoriate the skin around the anus.

d)   **PROCTITIS. Inflammation of the rectum.** This usually arises as a result of the presence of some mechanical object or foreign body, e.g. bone splinters. Inflammation can become severe in some cases and is attended by straining and possibly prolapse of the rectal lining. Examination of the rectal passage reveals the mucous membrane to be thickened and possibly ulcerated.

TREATMENT. The following remedies may bring relief and should be combined with a semi-fluid diet and the avoidance of bulky foods:

1.   COLLINSONIA 200c. Severe straining is present, accompanying constipation. Anal prolapse may occur. Dysenteric stools may alternate with hard motions.

2. PODOPHYLLUM 30c. Morning diarrhoea is associated with this remedy, the stools being greenish and profuse. Tendency to prolapse is pronounced. The internal mucous membranes feel lumpy and possibly ulcerated.

3. ALOE 200c. Stools are accompanied by much flatus and are jelly-like due to the presence of mucus. The anus may show excoriation.

4. RUTA 30c. Severe straining accompanies passage of stool and there is a strong tendency to rectal prolapse. The stools are usually fewer, although occasionally frothy mucoid evacuations will occur in severe cases.

e) **DIARRHOEA AND CONSTIPATION.** It will be convenient to deal with these two conditions under the general consideration of intestinal upsets.

Character of Stool. Stools may be watery, mucoid or dysenteric with varying degrees of consistency and colour. Large evacuations indicate that the source of the trouble is in the small intestine rather than the large. Small stools frequently evacuated may indicate colitis as does the presence of a large amount of mucus. Frothy stools which may contain fat globules frequently indicate pancreatitis or diabetes. Black stools indicate haemorrhages somewhere in the intestinal tract. Clay-coloured faeces are associated with liver dysfunction while the presence of orange pigment usually means that a leptospiral infection is present.

1. Diarrhoea. Reference has already been made to this condition under Entero-colitis and the remedies listed there are applicable to the treatment of diarrhoea in general. It must be emphasised, however, that these are among the more common ones and many more are available. It would be confusing to a beginner in homoeopathy to list them all and an overall symptom picture would be necessary in order to determine which one would be indicated.

2. Constipation. Retention of faeces can be mild or severe and has its origin in reduced fluid intake, the consumption of large amounts of bones and also to reflexes of one kind or another.

CLINICAL SIGNS. Severe straining accompanies passage of small hard lumps of stool, possibly containing blood. Vomiting is not uncommon and signs of posterior inco-ordination may arise in prolonged cases. The dog resents abdominal palpation.

TREATMENT. The following remedies are all useful according to the overall picture:

1. NUX VOM. 1M. There is frequent straining with passage of small amounts at a time. The origin of the trouble usually lies in a dietary upset and may be associated with vomiting. This is a good digestive remedy and will help regulate proper bowel movements.

2. SULPHUR 6c. When this remedy is indicated there is usually pronounced redness around the anus accompanied by much scratching in general. The body odour may be musty. It acts well in conjunction with the previous remedy.

3. BRYONIA 6c. Stools are large and dark coloured and passed more frequently in the morning. The animal is generally uneasy and is disinclined to move. Tenderness over the abdomen is very pronounced, although pressure is not resented.

4. ANT. CRUD. 6c. Hard lumpy stools are passed along with watery discharge and occasionally mucus. The mouth symptoms are frequently a good guide to its use, the tongue being white and eczematous eruptions forming near the lips.

5. OPIUM 200c. A most useful remedy for severe and obstinate cases. The general appearance of the animal may be comatose and lethargic. Stools are exceedingly hard and black.

6. LYCOPODIUM 1M. With the remedy there is usually a history of liver disturbance or an accompanying hepatitis. Stools are small and the appetite is capricious, very little satisfying. Lean or undernourished looking animals may respond well to this remedy, other symptoms agreeing.

7. ALUMEN 6c. This remedy may be indicated for the older animal showing a tendency to tissue induration. Constipation can be severe. There may be an associated alopecia and eczematous eruptions. Muscular weakness is usually present.

FOOTNOTE. As for diarrhoea these are only a few of the common remedies which may be needed.

6 DISEASES OF LIVER AND PANCREAS

a) THE LIVER. Conditions affecting the function of the liver may have their origin in bacterial or viral invasion or be due to a metabolic upset associated with faulty nutrition.

CLINICAL SIGNS OF GENERAL LIVER DISEASE. Palpation over the right abdominal area may reveal an enlarged liver and this is not always associated with pain. Vomiting and inappetance are usually present when there is liver dysfunction. The character of the stool is frequently a good guide to liver disturbance, the faeces being orange or clay-coloured. Jaundice is a sign that the liver is not functioning as it should and bile pigments may be deposited in the urine giving it a yellowish-green colour. Visible mucous membranes become yellow. Jaundice, however, is not always present when the function of the liver is disturbed. In chronic disease and in those associated with tumour formation, ascites (abdominal dropsy) is usually present.

TREATMENT OF LIVER CONDITIONS. This will be dependent on the overall symptom picture but there are certain remedies which have a selective action on liver function and they include the following:

1. CHELIDONIUM 6c. Indications for this remedy include a yellowish tongue and discoloration of visible mucous membranes. Vomiting is usually present and signs of stiffness or pain may be evident over the right shoulder region. Stools are clay-coloured.

2. PHOSPHORUS 200c. Vomiting is noticed shortly after the animal takes food or water and when it becomes warm in the stomach. Small haermorrhages may be seen on the gums. Hepatitis occurs and stools become pale and hard. The region over the liver becomes extremely tender on palpation.

3. CARDUUS MAR. 30c. Vomiting is again pronounced under this remedy. There is interference with bile distribution with consequent jaundice. Yellow stools occur while interference with portal circulation leads to abdominal dropsy. This is a useful remedy if cirrhosis is suspected.

4. CROTALUS HORR. 200c. This is an important remedy in cases of haemolytic jaundice with abdominal distension and possibly vomiting of blood. It has given good results in Leptospirosis and similar septicaemic conditions where an overall haemorrhagic tendency exists.

5. *AESCULUS 30c.* Jaundice is also associated with this remedy. The portal circulation becomes congested leading to signs of abdominal discomfort soon after eating. Tenderness occurs over the liver. Stools are large and hard, and the urine becomes discoloured. There may be accompanying respiratory symptoms such as coughing up of mucus.

6. *LYCOPODIUM 1M.* A prominent liver remedy, one of the main indications for its use being an inability to eat much at any one time. Very little food appears to satisfy. In addition all symptoms are aggravated in late afternoon and early evening. A suitable remedy for the old and the lean animal. Premature greying of the coat could be a further indication for its use. Stools are generally hard.

7. *HEPAR SULPH. 30c.* If liver abscess is suspected as a sequel to pyogenic infection, this remedy will generally help. There is sensitivity to touch and all external lesions are excessively painful.

8. *NUX VOM. 1M.* If liver dysfunction is secondary to overeating or partaking of unsuitable food, this remedy will be indicated. Stools are hard and the animal's temperament becomes uncertain.

If specific diseases such as Hepatitis and/or Leptospirosis have affected the liver, the use of the appropriate nosode will be indicated.

9. *MORGAN 30c.* This bowel nosode is a useful adjunct to the use of indicated remedies. It is indicated when there is general portal congestion leading to stasis of alimentary function.

10. *SULPHUR 200c.* Indicated when liver disturbance occurs in the dog which shows a dirty skin with redness of the skin around the anus and having a generally musty odour.

11. *MERC. DULC. 6c.* This is a principal liver remedy indicated in chronic liver upsets showing jaundice and ascites. Stools are slimy and mucoid with a dark-greenish colour due to bile pigments, but are passed without straining (unlike *MERC. CORR.*).

12. *BERBERIS VUL. 6c.* This remedy is associated with the production of gall-stones and a tendency to urolithiasis. Bile function is interfered with and stools become clay-coloured. Jaundice may or may not be present but if it is the urine becomes dark yellow.

13. *CHIONANTHUS 30c.* Also a good remedy. Should be considered if the above remedies fail to give good results.

b) THE PANCREAS. This gland is important in two main respects:
1. for the control of carbohydrate metabolism through its hormone insulin and
2. for the production of enzymes which help to digest protein and fat.

PANCREATITIS. Inflammation of the pancreas may be acute or chronic.

a) **Acute Form.** This is often seen in the overfat dog which has been fed an unbalancd diet of low protein and high fat but lean animals are also at risk.

CLINICAL SIGNS. Arching of the back is a common sign and the abdominal muscles become hard. Attacks may come on suddenly and give rise to a state of shock. Temperature is at first raised but in severe cases tends to fall, producing coldness of the body surface. Vomiting is usually severe and if not checked leads to dehydration. Pressure on the abdomen elicits pain. Stools are frothy and may contain fat globules. Increased thirst is evident.

TREATMENT. The following remedies have proved useful in practice:

1. IRIS VERS. 30c. This is one of the most important remedies. Vomiting may contain bile and stools become watery and greenish. Abdominal pain is severe.

2. ATROPINUM 6c. The alkaloid Belladonna has a selective action on the pancreas and could be indicated in those cases associated with a dry mouth and inability to swallow properly. Vomiting relieves symptoms and the umbilical area is extremely sensitive to touch.

3. CHIONANTHUS 6c. This is a good general pancreatic remedy indicated when there are accompanying liver derangements showing clay-coloured stools and tenderness over the hepatic region. Abdominal pain is severe.

4. IODUM 6c. Stools are consistently frothy and fatty when this remedy is indicated. Suitable for the lean animal which shows a voracious appetite and dry coat. Jaundice may be present.

5. PANCREAS 30c. The Pancreas nosode will be of use in association with other indicated remedies.

6. MORGAN 30c. This bowel nosode aids by helping the digestive system generally. It should be used prior to the introduction of the selected remedy.

7. ACONITUM 12x. Suitable for the attack which comes on suddenly and will be indicated in the early high temperature stage.

b) **Chronic Form.** This may be associated with fibrous induration of pancreatic tissue and sometimes occurs as a sequel to the acute form.

CLINICAL SIGNS. The appetite is usually maintained and in many instances becomes excessive. Despite this, however, the animal suffers a progressive loss of weight. Thirst is also increased. A distinctive sign is the production of a massive faecal bulk which is greyish in colour and fatty in consistency. Abdominal pain may be present but is not a constant sign.

TREATMENT. The following remedies have all proved useful according to individual symptoms:

1. IODUM 30c. This remedy is associated with voracious appetite and an inability to gain weight. It is well-adapted to lean animals with dry, harsh coats. Stools are frothy and contain fat globules. Lymphatic glands are often hard and smaller than usual.

2. SILICEA 30c. If it is suspected that fibrous tissue induration is present, this remedy should prove useful. It has a deserved reputation in reducing scar or fibrous tissue and will aid a return to normal function.

3. BARYTA MUR. 30c. This is a useful remedy for the older animal. Tonsillar tissue is frequently enlarged causing difficulty in swallowing, and there may be intermittent vomiting.

4. APOCYNUM CANN. 30c. Dropsical conditions, especially ascites, are usually present when this remedy is indicated. Thirst is markedly increased and there may be excessive vomiting.

5. IRIS VERS. 30c. As in the acute form, Iris will also be found of benefit in the chronic state. Stools are watery, frothy and greenish in colour and there is tenderness over the stomach area.

6. MORGAN 30c. An intercurrent dose of this bowel nosode will be useful in supplementing the action of selected remedies.

7. PHOSPHORUS 30c. There is usually an accompanying Hepatitis when this remedy is indicated. Stools are clay-coloured and sago-like. Small haemorrhages may appear on the mucous membranes of mouth.

THE PERITONEUM. Inflammation of the peritoneal membrane may be acute or chronic.

a) Acute Form. The most likely cause of this in the dog is some form of external injury causing penetration of the abdominal wall and subsequent inflammation. Secondary infection arises as a result of the entrance of pyogenic organisms with the result that abscess formation develops.

CLINICAL SIGNS. There is an initial rise in temperature, followed by vomiting and increased passage of stool which, however, later becomes reduced due to a lack of bowel activity. The abdominal muscles become rigid giving a board-like feeling and causing the animal to stand with arched back probably in an attempt to relieve pain which is severe. The animal may cry out when palpated over the abdomen. The expression is anxious. Examination of blood reveals a large increase in the number of white cells.

TREATMENT. If the attack is noticed early and before severe symptoms arise, the following remedies should prove useful:

1. ACONITUM 6x. Always give this remedy as soon as the condition is suspected. Guiding symptoms which will reinforce its selection include anxiety and signs of shock. The pulse will be hard and wiry.

2. BELLADONNA 200c. Indications for this remedy include dilated pupils, excessive body heat, redness of the oral mucosa and a full bounding pulse. The mouth is dry and there may be hawking from the throat. In severe cases convulsions may arise when this remedy is called for.

3. COLOCYNTHIS 30c. Abdominal pain is severe and initial stools are watery or jelly-like and are worse after drinking. One of the chief indications for its use is an arched back which may be so excessive as to give the appearance of the dog bending double.

4. HEPAR SULPH. 30c. If abscess formation is suspected possibly because of an increased white cell count, this remedy will prove useful.

Inguinal lymph glands are invariably swollen and in severe cases may burst, liberating pus. The animal is extremely susceptible to pain and touch when this remedy is needed.

5. *BRYONIA 30c.* This particular remedy is indicated generally in inflammations affecting serous surfaces. The animal will be unwilling to move and may lie flat with the abdomen pressed against the ground. Any movement aggravates all symptoms.

6. *MERC. CORR. 200c.* Indicated when the initial stool takes the form of a mucoid dysentery, symptoms becoming worse in the period from sunset to sunrise. Mouth symptoms such as ulceration and salivation may be present.

7. *ARSEN. ALB. 1M.* Indicated for restless patients which drink frequently and show a deterioration of symptoms towards midnight. The coat is harsh and dry and vomiting is severe. The initial stool is dark, watery and cadaverous.

8. *APIS MEL. 30c.* The initial inflammation is usually attended by oedema and this remedy may give good results in the early stages for this reason. It is rarely indicated later unless generalised oedema appears.

9. *RHUS TOX. 1M.* Animals tend to move about which appears to minimise symptoms. Redness of mouth and throat are present and signs of abdominal pain are severe, especially in the lower bowel area. There may be a vesicular rash over the abdominal area.

10. *CALC. FLUOR. 30c.* As this remedy limits the tendency for adhesions to form, it is good practice to give a course of it after an acute attack.

b) Chronic Form. This usually arises as a result of a previous acute attack. The lesions which develop as a result of this give rise to adhesions which are the main accompaniment of the chronic state. Treatment is purely symptomatic and includes particularly the remedies *HEPAR SULPH. 30c*, *SILICEA 30c* and *CALC. FLUOR. 30c*.

   HEPAR. should be given if there is a flare-up of symptoms giving rise to enlarged lymphatic glands in the inguinal region and suspected abscess formation. *SILICEA* will help reduce fibrosis in any adhesions present and will also be useful in controlling a chronic suppurative state. *CALC. FLUOR.* is a good remedy for the early indurated process and will greatly limit the tendency to fresh adhesions forming.

ASCITES. By this term is meant the presence in the abdominal cavity of an excess amount of fluid and associated with various clinical states, particularly heart and liver complaints. Abscesses and tumours may also play a part.

CLINICAL SIGNS. There is obvious enlargement of the abdomen with an absence of pain. The presence of excess fluid brings about pressure on the diaphragm with resultant embarrassment of breathing. To relieve this the animal assumes an upright seated posture throwing as much weight as possible on to the lower abdomen. Percussion over the abdominal wall may reveal a splashing sound when extensive amounts are present. A general loss of condition usually accompanies the condition from whatever cause.

TREATMENT. The basic cause must be determined and treatment directed towards that end, e.g. heart remedies may be indicated as well as those influencing the liver. Remedies which favourably influence the heart's action act by increasing the volume of blood and promoting increased circulation. This in turn reduces the amount of fluid in the abdomen. These include the following:

1. CRATAEGUS 1x. One of the best remedies for stimulating the heart muscle and strengthening the beat. It may have to be given as a long term cure.

2. ADONIS VER. 1x. One of the most useful heart remedies for ascites. Dyspnoea is usually marked. The heart's action is irregular with a rapid pulse.

3. CONVALLARIA 1x. Regulates the heart's action and is suitable for fluid retention generally.

4. DIGITALIS 6c. Indicated when the heart's action is slow and output of blood is consequently low. Causes increased urination by increasing the circulation generally.

If ascites is thought to be due to liver dysfunction, the following remedies may help:

1. CARDUUS MAR. 30c. A good general remedy when the trouble is dependent on cirrhosis or portal congestion. There may be an associated jaundice.

35

2. CHELIDONIUM 6c. Stools are clay-coloured or if jaundice is present they may be golden yellow. The urine is also discoloured. Signs of pain may be present over the right shoulder region. The eyes are muddy and a degree of conjunctivitis may be present.

3. LYCOPODIUM 1M. This remedy could be indicated in those cases which develop slowly as a result of prolonged weakness of liver function. More adapted to lean animals with poor digestion. The ascites will probably have been due to an acute hepatitis at some time when this remedy is indicated. The dog may show a premature greying particularly around around the muzzle.

4. AESCULUS 30c. This remedy is associated with protal and pelvic congestions with consequent venous stasis leading to a degree of ascites which could be severe in prolonged involvement. There are often accompanying respiratory symptoms due also to venous congestion in the thorax.

Other remedies which have given good results in the control of ascites include the following:

1. ACETIC ACID 30c. There is usually marked wasting and debility present. Visible mucous membranes are pale due to anaemia, and the heart action is weak. A degree of flatulence or tympany is present along with the ascites. Stools are watery and are passed more in the morning.

2. ABROTANUM 1x. Indicated when ascites is due to the presence of worms and there is an accompanying loss of flesh in the lower limbs. It has given good results in the treatment of ascites, especially when used in conjunction with Crataegus.

3. APOCYNUM CANN. 6c. This remedy is associated with an increase in secretions of mucous membranes and has a weakening effect on heart rate. It gives good results in ascites due to kidney disease.

4. PRUNUS SPINOSA 6c. This also relates to ascites due to a weakened kidney function and there is usually difficulty in expelling urine.

5. HELLEBORUS. 6c. Generalised weakness and muscular debility are associated with this remedy. There is a tendency to paresis because of the excessive weakness. Gurgling sounds of water may be heard in the abdomen.

Diseases of the Respiratory System

Many diseases of the respiratory system are part of the overall picture of specific diseases, e.g. Distemper, and reference should be made to these under the appropriate heading. Respiratory ailments developing in the absence of such diseases are relatively uncommon and arise more often as an accompaniment of breed anatomy and structure of various parts, e.g Greyhounds and Great Danes may be more disposed to pneumonia because of small or narrow thoracic capacity, while breeds such as the French Bulldog and Pekingese exhibit upper respiratory, especially nasal, trouble. The following conditions are the ones most likely to be encountered in the species as a whole:

1. RHINITIS

This is the name given to inflammation of the nasal mucous membrane and occurs only rarely as a separate entity. It is more often an accompaniment to specific disease.

ETIOLOGY. The inflammatory process is usually started by some irritant factor, but secondary infection soon sets in which changes the character of the discharge. Staphylococcal organisms are usually implicated in these cases.

CLINICAL SIGNS. Nasal discharge is a constant sign. This starts as serous and thin, becoming in stages mucous and finally muco-purulent. Streaks of blood may be present. The discharge may be acrid, in which case excoriation of the nostrils will be seen, and when persistent muco-purulent discharges are present they impede breathing because of obstruction of nostrils.

TREATMENT. Various useful remedies are available for the relief of rhinitis and these include the following more commonly used:

1. ARSEN. ALB. 30c. This is a useful remedy in the early stages when the discharge is thin and excoriating. There may be an accompanying watery discharge from the eyes in subjects who need this remedy, and also the patient may be thirsty for small quantities of water and have a dry, staring coat.

2. *PULSATILLA 30c*. Mild-tempered animals showing changeable moods may respond well to this remedy, the discharge being thick and creamy. There may be ulceration of the nostril area, and small streaks of blood may show.

3. *MERCURIUS 6c*. The discharge associated with this remedy assumes a greenish tinge and may contain blood. The nasal bones are frequently swollen. The remedy should be used either in the metallic form — *SOLUBILIS* — or as the *CORROSIVUS* salt.

4. *ALLIUM CEPA 6c*. Discharges are usually thin and watery accompanied by sneezing and lachrymation when this remedy is indicated. It could be useful in the very early stages.

5. *KALI IOD. 30c*. A useful remedy for those cases where the discharge becomes impacted and there is an attempt to sneeze which is usually ineffectual. Watering of the eyes is a prominent accompanying symptom.

6. *KALI BICH. 6c*. Discharges assume a bright yellow colour and develop into small plugs which have a tough, stringy appearance. Streaks of blood are often present.

7. *ACID. FLUOR. 30c*. If the nasal septum is suspected as a cause, e.g. ulceration, this remedy may help indirectly by aiding the healing process.

2. EPISTAXIS

Nose bleeding is rarely seen as an independent condition in the dog, most cases being due to mechanical injury. Occasionally it follows severe inflammatory lesions affecting the turbinate bones or upper nasal mucous membranes. The presence of tumours in the nasal cavity may also give rise to bleeding.

TREATMENT. With the exception of nasal tumours, which are more properly the field of surgery, the following remedies have all proved effective according to the nature of the bleeding and other symptoms displayed:

1. ACONITUM 6c. Indicated in spontaneous haemorrhages of bright red blood, which could be the result of exposure to severe cold or shock of some kind.

2. FICUS RELIGIOSA 6c. This remedy covers haemorrhages of whatever source and may be associated with bleeding from other parts as well as the nose.

3. PHOSPHORUS 30c. Associated with small capillary bleeding from the nasal mucous membrane rather than with larger flow of blood.

4. CROTALUS HORR. 30c. The snake venoms as a group are associated with haemolysis and bleeding takes place from many sources. The blood shows a tendency to remain fluid.

5. VIPERA 30c. This has an action somewhat similar to the previous remedy, but has a greater reputation in controlling nasal bleeding. The animal may show a tendency to vertigo when this remedy is indicated.

6. MELILOTUS 30c. The blood is bright-red and may accompany a feverish state. Frequently the blood will coagulate in the nostrils and can be removed as firm plugs.

7. IPECACUANHA 30c. This remedy also produces bright-red nasal bleeding in its provings. The animal which will benefit from its use may have accompanying gastric symptoms such as persistent vomiting.

8. FERRUM PHOS. 6c. When this remedy is indicated, the subject is usually a puppy and again the blood is bright-red with possibly an attendant feverish condition. Throat symptoms such as difficulty in swallowing may be present.

3. SINUSITIS

The maxillary sinus, or antrum as it is sometimes called, occasionally becomes the seat of infection or inflammation resulting in a collection of purulent material within the sinus.

ETIOLOGY. Infection may spread to the sinus from other areas of the upper respiratory tract, but the commonest source is an infected tooth.

CLINICAL SIGNS. The infective process eventually leads to a softening of the bone covering the maxillary sinus and ulceration of the skin ensues. A small hole thus develops which yields purulent material.Infection of a frontal sinus usually results in a purulent nasal discharge which becomes streaked with blood. There is usually an accompanying conjunctivitis.

TREATMENT. The radical care for sinusitis due to infected teeth is extraction of the offending tooth. Once this has been done the following remedies will help to treat the sinus lining and remove residual infection:

1. HEPAR SULPH. 30c. This remedy is indicated where there is pain and sensitivity over the affected area. Low potencies will promote expulsion of any residual pus, while high potencies will provide healing by granulation.

2. SILICEA 30c. Indicated in long-standing cases where the symptoms are less sensitive. It will help the healing process by drying any discharge and removing scar tissue.

3. ACID. FLUOR. 30c. This remedy will have a beneficial action on the sinus lining and will strengthen the maxillary bone where it has become weakened.

4. HECLA LAVA 12c. A specific action is exerted on the bones of the upper jaw by this remedy and its use will greatly assist the healing of diseased tissue. There may be an accompanying swelling of associated neck glands on the affected site.

5. HIPPOZAENINUM 30c. This nosode has proved of value in the treatment of infections of the frontal sinus showing purulent nasal discharge.

4. TONSILLITIS

Inflammation of tonsillar tissue can be either acute or chronic and is of fairly common occurrence.

a) Acute Form. This is associated with infection, mainly streptococcal, although other bacteria and also viruses can play a part.

CLINICAL SIGNS. The affected tissue becomes swollen and reddened due to increased blood supply and may show small greyish spots of necrosis and frothy exudate. Sometimes these foci coalesce to produce a membrane which covers the tonsils. The appetite may be variable but any attempts at swallowing are attended with discomfort. There may be an increase in the amount of saliva which can be clear or mucoid. Retching is a frequent accompaniment with vomiting of any excess mucus. A rise of temperature is usual in the early stages, particularly in puppies.

TREATMENT

1. *ACONITUM 6c.* This remedy should be given as early as possible when it will probably prevent the trouble developing further.

2. *MERC. CYANATUS 30c.* The mercury salts generally have a beneficial effect on mouth and throat conditions and this one in particular has a specific action on the throat. It is indicated where greyish membranes are evident and the mouth as a whole has a dirty look.

3. *MERC. SOL. 6c.* When there is an abundance of ropy saliva present together with ulcerations of gums and tonsil area, this remedy may be used effectively.

4. *PHYTOLACCA 30c.* Indicated where the tonsils are enlarged and the throat has a dark-red colour. Membranous deposits may be present, along with yellowish mucus.

5. *BELLADONNA 30c.* A useful remedy along with *ACONITUM* in the early stages. The patient may show excitability with dilated pupils and a full throbbing pulse.

6. *RHUS TOX. 6c.* The throat shows large amounts of mucus and assumes an unnaturally red colour. Externally the throat may be swollen. There may be accompanying eye symptoms, such as lachrymation, and generalised stiffness.

7. *APIS MEL. 6c.* Excessive oedema of tonsillar tissue indicates the use for this remedy. Warm drinks may aggravate the condition and a generalised swelling of the tonsillar area is present.

8. *KALI IOD. 30c.* The associated submaxillary glands and the thyroid gland may be affected when this remedy is indicated. Tonsils become red and swollen and there is an accompanying lachrymation.

9. *PHOSPHORUS 30c.* Excessive dryness of the tonsillar tissue may indicate this remedy. There are usually constitutional symptoms present such as vomiting and nervousness. The gums show small haemorrhages.

10. MERC. IOD. RUB. 30c. This remedy has a specific action on the left tonsillar area and is indicated when the other mercury symptoms, such as ulceration and salivation, etc. are present.

11. MERC. IOD. FLAV. 30c. The mercurous salt of iodine and mercury exerts action on the right-hand tonsillar area.

12. STREPTOCOCCUS 30c. An intercurrent dose of this nosode will help if the condition is thought to be of streptococcal origin. It can be used along with any other selected remedy.

b) Chronic Form. This can be a sequel to Distemper or some other infective process from which the animal has recovered. The tonsils are enlarged and become the seat of acute exacerbations which disappear under treatment but may tend to recur. Recurrence of this nature is less likely under homoeopathic medication and the following remedies will help to control this:

1. SILICEA 30c. This remedy will promote absorption of any fibrous or scar tissue which may be present and will also control any tendency to suppuration.

2. and 3. MERC. IOD. RUB. and FLAV. 30c. The red and yellow salts of mercury and iodine will have a similar action as indicated under the acute form.

4. BARYTA CARB. 6c. Both very young and old subjects will benefit from this remedy. There is a marked tendency to suppuration of the tonsillar tissue.

5. CALC. IOD. 30c. This remedy has proved extremely useful in chronic tonsillitis where the tonsils remain enlarged and become pitted with superficial ulcers. The patient is likely to be lean with a dry, staring coat.

6. HEPAR SULPH. 30c. Tonsils which periodically show purulent infection may be helped by this remedy. The throat becomes extremely painful and sensitive to pressure during these acute exacerbations.

7. KALI BICH. 6c. Swollen tonsils becoming ulcerated and yielding a yellow stringy pus are indications for this remedy. The tissue assumes a reddish-coppery tinge.

8. STREPTOCOCCUS NOSODE 30c. This nosode can profitably be combined with any of the foregoing remedies.

5. LARYNGITIS

Inflammation of the larynx may be acute or chronic.

a) Acute Form. This is usually associated with infection which may be primary or the result of having spread from neighbouring tissue. It is rarely systemic. Some authorities have attributed the condition to excessive or prolonged barking.

CLINICAL SIGNS. The quality of the bark becomes altered, a hoarse growl being emitted instead of the normal sound. This sound may be produced by palpation of the larynx. Excessive mucus of a frothy nature is present.

TREATMENT. The animal should be kept in a quiet place and one or other of the following remedies administered:

1. ACONITUM 6c. If given early in the disease, the symptoms will be abated and the process halted.

2. BELLADONNA 30c. Indicated for the animal which shows excitability, full bounding pulse and throbbing arteries. Can be profitably combined with the previous remedy.

3. APIS MEL. 30c. If the inflammation process is attended with much oedema and throat-swelling, this remedy should help. There is aversion to warmth in any form.

4. MERC. IOD. 30c. The red and yellow forms of this mercury salt may be indicated according to the location of the inflammatory lesions, e.g. if the right-hand laryngeal area is involved the yellow (*FLAVUS*) salt is indicated while the red (*RUBRUM*) favours the left.

5. SPONGIA TOSTA 6c. Indicated in the laryngeal conditions attended by a hoarse croupous cough. There is an absence of mucus. The respiration may be attended by a whistling sound.

6. DROSERA 9c. Spasmodic cough associated with the upper trachea and larynx indicates this remedy. Hoarseness is very pronounced, as also is tenacious mucus. The cough usually produces retching and vomiting in the dog, and greatly impedes proper breathing.

7. CAUSTICUM 30c. Indicated in those cases where the bark becomes lost due to a temporary paralysis of the laryngeal nerves. Coughing and hoarseness are both pronounced, attended by mucus. The cough may excite urination. Due to the attendant paralysis, the mucus gathers in the throat and the animal is unable to expel it.

8. LACHESIS 30c. Marked swelling of the throat region, worse on the left side, may indicate the need for this remedy. This swelling may impede breathing. There is a constant irritant cough usually without expectoration which is worse during the day and appears to be more constant after sleep.

9. RHUS TOX. 6c. Indicated when the larynx is deep red and the cough is attended by greenish mucus with a putrid smell. Occasionally blood is present in the expectoration or cough. A generalised stiffness of muscles and joints may be present which disappears on exercise.

b) Chronic Form. This develops as a sequel to maltreated acute cases and is characterised by hypertrophy of laryngeal tissue, often with a membranous deposit covering the larynx. It is associated with the production of oedema and swelling of the throat. Narrowing of the laryngeal opening may develop in severe cases.

TREATMENT. This follows much the same lines as for the acute form, but in addition the following remedies will help:

1. SILICEA 30c. This remedy helps promote healing of fibrous tissue and will hasten absorption of scar tissue. In addition it will guard against infection arising.

2. CALC. FLUOR. 30c. This is a good general tissue remedy and will help allay development of fibrous tissue.

3. PHYTOLACCA 30c. Useful in those cases where a membranous deposit covers the affected area. Marked redness of the larynx is the rule.

4. BARYTA MUR. 6c. A varicose condition of the throat veins is usually present when this remedy is indicated. There is a tendency to suppuration.

6.   KENNEL COUGH. TRACHEOBRONCHITIS

This is an inflammatory condition of the lower respiratory tract which usually results in a widespread infection and can spread with great rapidity when large numbers of dogs congregate. Carrier animals can occur and hence the condition soon becomes enzootic.

ETIOLOGY. There is usually a multiplicity of infective agents associated with this condition but probably viruses of the adeno group are the most likely causative agents.

CLINICAL SIGNS. Coughing is a constant sign, the type of cough being described as hacking. It is usually short in duration and dry in quality but occasionally a succession of short coughs develops which produces a paroxysmal effect. Symptoms are confined to the upper respiratory area and systemic involvement is extremely uncommon.

TREATMENT. There is a superficial resemblance to whooping cough in man and as in that disease the remedy *1. DROSERA 9c.* will be found to have good effect. Also to be considered are the following:

2.   PHOSPHORUS 30c. Indicated in dry cough with flecks of blood appearing in the nasal passages. The animal may show excitability. Rapid breathing with threatened pneumonia may occur.

3.   BRYONIA 30c. The pleurae become involved when this remedy is indicated. Breathing becomes of the abdominal type because of pain in the intercostal muscles. Pressure over the chest relieves symptoms and the animal prefers rest.

4.   SPONGIA TOSTA 6c. The cough is of the harsh dry variety, sometimes hoarse, and a whistling sound may be present. It may be associated with accompanying weak heart action.

5.   RUMEX 6c. The cough is attended by much mucus and is relieved in the evening or during the night. The character of the cough changes frequently.

6.   ACONITUM 6c. Should be given as early as possible in the infection when it will help allay development. It will also ease the condition by calming the animal and is especially useful in the evening for this purpose.

7. *SQUILLA MARITIMA 6c.* The animal usually takes deep breaths which brings on coughing when Scilla is needed as a remedy. Any exertion produces breathlessness. There are usually accompanying symptoms of lachrymation and sneezing with copious nasal secretion. The cough may produce reddish mucus, and is much worse in the morning.

8. *IPECACUANHA 30c.* Coughing produces reflex vomiting which can be frequent. The cough is worse at night. The change to a cold atmosphere can excite the cough. Blood may show in both the vomit and the expectoration from the cough. The respiration has been described as 'sighing'.

9. *COCCUS CACTI 6c.* Symptoms are worse at night and produce difficult respiration. Coughing can be continuous for many minutes, but sometimes alternating with long spells of relief.

10. *BROMIUM 6c.* There is much rattling of mucus in the upper trachea and larynx with this remedy. Inspiration is difficult and coughing may lead to fainting attacks because of lack of breath. The cough is wheezing and rough.

11. *CARBO VEG. 30c.* There is pronounced air hunger with this remedy and the animal seeks the cool open air. Cough in the morning produces expectoration of greenish-yellow pus. The breath is cold. Cough becomes worse in the evening. This is an extremely valuable remedy for those animals which show acute respiratory distress at night and usually gives immediate relief.

FOOTNOTE. An oral vaccine is available for the protection of dogs against Kennel Cough and can also be used for treatment in conjunction with other remedies.

7. CHRONIC BRONCHITIS

This may follow an acute attack of Kennel Cough or be a sequel to some other infectious disease of a systemic nature, probably viral. It is also seen in older animals accompanying heart weakness.

CLINICAL SIGNS. The cough in this condition differs from that in acute tracheo-bronchitis in being mucoid instead of dry. It is rarely of a purulent nature and can be easily excited by extraneous factors, e.g. by frequent movement, exercise and palpation of chest and throat. Thus the symptoms tend to be ameliorated at rest.

TREATMENT

1. BRYONIA 30c. Indicated when the animal appears to be better by resting. Deep pressure over the pleural region gives relief.

2. KALI BICH. 6c. This is a useful remedy where excess secretion is present, the animal having difficulty in raising mucus. There may be an accompanying nasal discharge. In long-standing cases the secretion becomes yellow.

3. ANTIMONIUM TART. 30c. Indicated when coughing is frequent and the discharge is frothy and mucoid.

4. APIS MEL. 6c. When excess fluid is suspected, leading to pulmonary congestion, this remedy should help.

5. SPONGIA TOSTA 6c. A useful remedy in the older animal when there are accompanying symptoms of heart involvement.

6. RUMEX 6c. This also is a good remedy in heart conditions which accompany bronchitis.

7. SQUILLA MARITIMA 6c. When this remedy is indicated there are usually symptoms of gastric involvement, e.g. vomiting and reflex coughing.

8. KREOSOTUM 30c. This is also a useful remedy in long-standing cases where secondary infection arises shown by purulent exudate being coughed up.

9. COCCUS CACTI 6c. A good remedy in the earlier stages where the cough is of a spasmodic nature and is worse at night.

8. BRONCHIECTASIS

This is the term used to describe the bronchial tree when it becomes abnormally dilated due to a loss of tone or elasticity in its fibres. This allows fluids to develop in pockets which eventually become receptacles for purulent material.

ETIOLOGY. It is frequently a sequel to some other pulmonary disease but it can also arise as a result of foreign bodies being aspirated into the lung. The primary disease is bacterial or viral in origin.

CLINICAL SIGNS. Continual coughing is the usual premonitory sign and while this is dry and unproductive in the early stages it soon becomes moist and the patient coughs up large quantities of muco-purulent material and loss of condition attends these symptoms.

TREATMENT

1. ANTIMONIUM TART 30c. A useful remedy in the early stages when the cough is attended by frothy exudate.

2. HEPAR SULPH. 30c. This is a good remedy in the early purulent stages and will limit the risk of secondary bacterial involvement.

3. HIPPOZAENINUM 30c. This nosode is useful in controlling the spread of infection to other parts of the respiratory tract.

4. KALI BICH. 30c. Indicated when the cough is accompanied by tough mucus of a yellow stringy nature.

5. KREOSOTUM 30c. A useful remedy in long-standing cases when gangrenous changes are threatened. The expectoration is extremely putrid and may be tinged with blood.

6. STAPHYLOCOCCUS 30c. Indicated if it is thought the Staphylococcal organisms may be present as a result of some previous infection of this nature.

7. STREPTOCOCCUS 30c. Likewise if Streptococcal involvement is suspected.

8. TUB. AVIARE 30c. This nosode is very useful in bronchial conditions which are slow to heal and can usefully be employed along with other selected remedies.

9. MALANDRINUM 30c. This is another useful nosode which can be combined with other remedies. Mucus tends to be honey-coloured and sticky.

10. MERC. SOL. 6c. This remedy could be indicated when any material coughed up is of a greenish rather than of a yellow colour.

Diseases of the Lungs and Pleura

1. PULMONARY OEDEMA

The abnormal accumulation of fluid in the lung is usually a sequel to chronic heart disease, especially mitral valve insufficiency when the weakness of the circulation causes a transudation of blood plasma from the pulmonary veins into the lung tissue. It may also arise as a sequel to Distemper.

CLINICAL SIGNS. There is great difficulty in breathing and a wet cough is fairly constant. If it accompanies some other primary disease, signs of the latter are usually present also.

TREATMENT

1. APIS MEL. 30c. This remedy is always indicated when oedema is present in whatever situation.

2. CACTUS GRANDIFLORUS 6c. This is a good heart remedy which will stimulate the heart's action and thereby increase circulation. This will then reduce the likelihood of pulmonary stasis developing in a serious form.

3. ADONIS VERNALIS. 6c. This is also a good heart remedy which should have a beneficial effect in valvular disease.

4. CRATAEGUS Ø or 1x or 6c. A heart remedy which exerts its action on the muscle thereby increasing the force of the beat and leading to greater output of blood. In this way circulation as a whole is stimulated.

5. CARBO VEG. 30c. This is a useful remedy which gives relief by helping the patient's oxygen supply and thereby aiding breathing in general.

6. ABROTANUM 6c. This remedy has a reputation for aiding conditions which give rise to exudations in general. It is therefore likely to help lung congestions if other selected symptoms are present.

7. VERATRUM VIR. 30c. This is another useful remedy in valvular heart conditions and will thereby help circulatory weakness.

2. EMPHYSEMA

When the alveoli of the lungs lose their elasticity, becoming distended and unable to return to their normal size, a state of emphysema is said to exist. In severe cases the alveolar wall may rupture permitting the escape of air into the surrounding tissues.

ETIOLOGY. It is invariably a sequel to some chronic respiratory disorder such as bronchitis or bronchiectasis. Severe attacks of pneumonia will also predispose towards it.

CLINICAL SIGNS. There is obvious difficulty in expelling air and respiration may be associated with forced movements of the abdominal muscles in order to assist the process. There is general difficulty in breathing. Tension in the pulmonary vessels arises as a result of increased pressure on the right ventricle of the heart.

TREATMENT

1. ACONITUM 6c. Always indicated when there is tension in any part of the circulatory system and should give relief indirectly as a result.

2. LOBELIA INFLATA 30c. This remedy has proved useful in the treatment of functional emphysema where the changes in the alveolar walls have not proceeded too far or have become chronic.

3. ANTIMONIUM ARSEN. 30c. This is a useful remedy when examination reveals that the left lung is affected more than the right.

4. CARBO VEG. 30c. Will provide oxygen by its ability to help in cases of 'air hunger'. It will give relief particularly at night.

The above remedies and treatments refer to cases of functional emphysema where damage to the alveoli is partial. Structural emphysema where the tone or elasticity of the alveolar wall is completely lost is unlikely to prove responsive to treatment.

3. PNEUMONIA

Inflammation of the lung substance can take various forms, chief among which are Broncho-pneumonia and Hypostatic pneumonia.

BRONCHO-PNEUMONIA. This is the infective type of pneumonia which is associated with viral or bacterial disease and, apart from the virus of Distemper, various species of Streptococci and other bacteria are implicated.

CLINICAL SIGNS. There is an initial rise of temperature followed by a nasal discharge of muco-purulent material which may be streaked with blood. Respirations are increased and in severe cases dyspnoea is evident. Coughing is a fairly constant sign and, if bacterial or viral invasion is thought to have taken place, other systemic signs may appear, e.g. vomiting and constipation. The animal becomes dehydrated and unkempt and water intake is decreased.

TREATMENT. The following remedies are all useful according to type and symptoms displayed:

1. ACONITUM 6c. Should always be given as early in the condition as possible.

2. ANTIMONIUM TART. 30c. A very useful remedy when there is an abundance of loose mucus and expectoration.

3. BRYONIA 6c. When this remedy is indicated the animal resents movement. Pressure over the affected area brings relief. The animal prefers to lie on the affected side.

4. ARSEN. IOD. 6c. A good remedy for the less severe case or one which is of a recurrent nature. Symptoms may be worse at night and the skin is dry with a harsh coat.

5. FERRUM PHOS. 6c. The animal may show signs of pain and anxiety when breathing in. There is an abundance of loose mucus in the throat. Coughing may produce blood, and is associated with distress.

6. LYCOPODIUM 30c. A useful remedy for lean animals with indifferent appetite. There may be aggravation of symptoms in late afternoon to early evening.

7. PHOSPHORUS 30c. Expectoration of rust-coloured sputum may accompany vomiting. Alternatively the cough may be dry and unproductive. A suitable remedy for nervous and sensitive animals.

8. TUBERCULINUM AVIARE 30c. This nosode has proved useful in convalescence when it will aid the healing process after administration of selected remedies.

4. HYPOSTATIC PNEUMONIA

This condition occurs in old dogs and also in those which are chronically run down and in poor health. If the animal is recumbent for any length of time the lack of exercise and general weakness permits plasma transudate to gravitate towards the lungs producing a pneumonia of this type.

CLINICAL SIGNS. There is great difficulty in breathing and coughing is again present. The signs of pneumonia will be more evident on the side on which the animal is lying. The cough is usually dry.

TREATMENT. The animal should be turned over frequently and encouraged to take mild exercise if possible. Remedies which are helpful include the following:

1.   APIS MEL. 30c. This remedy will help in removing excess fluid and reducing the tendency to oedema in general.

2.   ADONIS VER. 1x and CONVALLARIA 1x are useful heart remedies which should stimulate the heart's action and increase the circulation. This will apply to other heart remedies also as discussed under Congestive Heart Disease.

5. PLEURA. Pleurisy

Inflammation of the pleural membranes may be either dry or accompanied by effusion into the pleural sac.

ETIOLOGY. Usually the cause is due to extension of infection from some part of the respiratory tract, although a primary cause may also occur less frequently e.g. by trauma.

CLINICAL SIGNS. The animal appears anxious and signs of abdominal breathing are present, signifying pain on inspiration. If one side only is affected the animal seeks to lie on that side, whereas if the animal assumes a sitting position it usually indicates affection of both sides. The temperature may rise to 105°F. and accompanies early signs of pain. If effusion occurs signs of pain may be less. Auscultation in the dry form reveals a harsh friction sound, but such sounds become less evident when effusion is present.

TREATMENT. The following remedies may be needed depending on overall symptoms:

1. ACONITUM 30c. Should always be given as early in the condition as possible. It will quickly allay anxiety and helps relieve pain.

2. BELLADONNA 30c. A useful remedy if the animal feels unduly hot with dilated pupils and throbbing pulses.

3. BRYONIA 6c or 30c. This is probably the best remedy to consider in the majority of cases once the condition is established. A main guiding principle for its use is relief of pain on pressure, seen by the animal lying on the affected side and disinclined to move.

4. APIS MEL. 30c. This remedy should help to reduce the fluid which is present in those cases showing effusion.

5. ARSEN. ALB. 30c. Older animals may benefit from this remedy especially if symptoms are worse towards midnight and the patient seeks small sips of water.

Diseases of the Nervous System

1. THE BRAIN AND MENINGES

Disturbances of the brain may be either functional or organic and we will look at each category separately. In the former there are no structural changes in the nervous tissue and such conditions in the dog are of less importance than those which fall into the organic category.

The main functional disorder of importance is a form of epilepsy which has no obvious cause. It is of fairly common occurrence.

CLINICAL SIGNS OF EPILEPSY. The owner's attention is first drawn to the occurrence of minor convulsions which last sometimes less than a minute and are usually unaccompanied by loss of consciousness. These attacks tend to become more serious but less frequent as the animal gets older. Attacks can come on suddenly without premonitory symptoms but occasionally the animal appears restless and uneasy immediately prior to the seizure and is lethargic and sleepy-looking afterwards.

TREATMENT. If there has been a history of short attacks which pass off quickly, the following remedies will help delay the onset of further seizures. They will also help during the actual attack, limiting it considerably.

1. BELLADONNA 30c. This is one of the most frequently indicated remedies, for attacks which are associated with dilated pupils and throbbing pulse. The animal will usually feel abnormally hot.

2. STRAMONIUM 30c. This remedy has a somewhat similar picture to the preceding one, but there are usually premonitory signs, such as staggering with a tendency to fall towards the left side. Eyes are again dilated and staring.

3. HYOSCYAMUS 30c. Indicated when attacks are preceded by shaking of the head and an unsteadiness of gait indicating vertigo. There may be spasmodic closing of eyelids and the mouth is flecked with foam.

4. BUFO 30c. The symptoms indicative of this remedy frequently commence when the animal is asleep. There may be an accompanying nose-bleed. Attacks are usually of short duration.

5. COCCULUS 6c. The main use for this remedy lies more in the preventive sphere and is useful to ward off subsequent attacks. It should be given at regular intervals over a period of a few months.

6. IGNATIA 6c. Consciousness is usually lost when this remedy is indicated. The head may be shaken to and fro and this precedes hysterical turns.

7. CUPRUM MET. 30c. A useful remedy when convulsions are associated more with meningitis than encephalitis. The head usually assumes a lowered posture and there may be attempts to press it against any suitable object.

8. CICUTA VIROSA 30c. This remedy also is associated with meningitis both cerebral and spinal. A prominent indication for its use is a turning of the head and neck to one side. There may be a history of concussion leading to convulsions.

9. OENANTHE CROCATA 6c. This lesser known remedy is associated with sudden convulsive attacks accompanied by twitching of the face and head muscles and symptoms suggestive of lock-jaw.

10. ABSINTHUM 6c. Indicated when attacks are preceded by excitement and twitchings of various kinds. The patient tends to face backwards and there may be unequal dilation of pupils.

FOOTNOTE. Some forms of epileptiform convulsions have their origin in conventional vaccination and the possibility of this should be borne in mind. If it is suspected that attacks date from such vaccination, the nosode Distemperinum or other appropriate one should be used in conjunction with selected remedies. Usually two doses of any nosode are sufficient, spacing them one week apart.

ORGANIC DISORDERS OF THE BRAIN

These include Hydrocephalus, Encephalitis and Meningitis.

1. HYDROCEPHALUS. This is the term given to the condition which arises as a result of an excess amount of fluid accumulating in the ventricles of the brain. The condition is not uncommon in small or toy breeds and may be congenital in many instances.

CLINICAL SIGNS. These vary according to the amount of fluid present. Convulsions of an epileptiform type may occur and occasionally the animal walks with a stumbling or knuckling action. Excessive drowsiness is a common feature and dilation of pupils is normally present. Exact diagnosis of the condition may necessitate X-ray or encephalographic examination.

TREATMENT. The following remedies may help according to the type of symptom displayed:

1. APIS MEL. 6c. This remedy should be given as a routine because of its association with oedema and excess fluid development. It should thus help to disperse the fluid which accumulates.

2. PHOSPHORUS 30c. This is one of the remedies which may help control vertigo-like symptoms in the older subject. The patient is usually restless and seeks warmth.

3. APOCYNUM CANN. 6c. This is a very useful remedy to try in this condition. Again vertigo is a prominent feature with pressing of right side of head against any suitable object. Sight is interfered with. The vertigo may disappear quickly and re-appear with equal suddenness.

4. HELLEBORUS NIGER 30c. As with the preceding remedies, giddiness is a constant feature. The animal has a stupefied look and may cry out with pain. The head is pressed against any suitable object and the body feels cold.

5. ARGENT. NIT. 6c. When this remedy is indicated symptoms of fear may be present. There is a tendency to fall sideways, and attacks of vertigo may be accompanied by vomiting of bile, and conjunctivitis of varying degree is sometimes seen.

6. CUPRUM ACETICUM 6c. Abdominal pain and signs of colic may accompany the usual vertigo-like symptoms, the animal showing thirst and frequent bowel evacuations. The passage of a stool frequently brings relief from other symptoms.

7. CALC. CARB. 30c. This is a remedy which may give relief in young pups, especially those of the brachycephalic breeds and those which are too fat.

8. CALC. PHOS. 30c. This is also indicated in the young subject but more in the leaner animal. It greatly assists bone development and will help overcome the pressure on the fontanelles which sometimes happens in severe cases of hydrocephalus.

9. ZINC. MUR. 30c. This is a very useful remedy to keep in mind when dealing with this condition. The attacks of vertigo lead to fainting fits, and the eyes have a sunken look. The limbs show tremors and spasmodic twitchings. Extreme restlessness is a main feature with inability to sleep.

2. ENCEPHALITIS. Inflammation of the brain substance is not uncommon and occurs in all breeds.

ETIOLOGY. The main causes are viruses and bacteria of different kinds, chief among which are the causative agents of Distemper and some strains of Streptococci. Bacterial spread from neighbouring infected areas such as sinuses and eyes and ears can also lead to encephalitis.

CLINICAL SIGNS. Varying degrees of nervous excitement are at first seen in mild cases, leading in more severe states to convulsions. The eyes are usually staring and have an anxious or wild expression. The conjunctivae are red. Choreic symptoms such as facial twitching and head-shaking may be present. The animal may cry out in pain. There is a staggering gait with stumbling and a tendency to fall forwards or backwards.

TREATMENT. The following remedies have given good results according to symptoms displayed:

1. BELLADONNA 30c. This is one of the chief remedies for relieving convulsions in the acute stage. Indications for its use are dilated pupils, throbbing pulse and redness of eyes.

2. ACONITUM 30c. If attacks come on suddenly this remedy will help allay shock and limit the scope of the attack. It should be alternated every half-hour with the previous remedy for a total of four doses each.

3. STRAMONIUM 30c. This remedy may be useful for the less acute case which shows a staggering gait with a tendency to fall towards the left side or even backwards. Abdominal symptoms such as colic and diarrhoea may accompany these attacks. Convulsive movements of the head are present and sight is usually lost.

4. *AGARICUS 6c.* Dizziness is a prominent indication for the use of this remedy. There are usually four recognised stages of cerebral excitement displayed, ranging from slight stimulation, muscular twitchings, symptoms and mental depression exhibited as lethargy. Convulsions are usually absent if this remedy is indicated.

5. *CICUTA VIROSA 30c.* When this remedy is indicated, a prominent feature is a turning of the head and neck to one side and frequently an S-bend is noticeable. Vomiting and diarrhoea may be present. Twitching of head muscles is present.

6. *TARENTULA HISPANICA 30c.* The animal which needs this remedy may show a deep mistrust of people or objects which normally would be taken on trust. Actions have been described as stealthy or 'foxy'. Fits of rage and extreme excitement may be present.

7. *OPIUM 30c.* When convulsions or fits are followed by excessive drowsiness this remedy is indicated. The bowels are extremely inactive. The eyes are half open and the pupils may be contracted.

8. *CONIUM MACULATUM 30c.* This remedy has a useful action in the older animal. Prominent among its indications are weakness of different kinds in the hind legs ranging from unsteady gait to an inability to rise with a progressive upwards paralysis.

9. *BUFO 6c.* Nose-bleeding often accompanies a convulsive attack when this remedy is indicated. These bleedings usually give relief. Noise and light aggravate the condition. Prior to an attack the head may be drawn backwards or to one side.

3. MENINGITIS. This condition may be associated with encephalitis or arise independently, and is usually associated with specific agents such as bacteria or viruses.

CLINICAL SIGNS. The dog is usually more aware of his surroundings and reacts to external stimuli more noticeably than a normal animal. The temperature is raised and the neck muscles become rigid causing the patient to keep the head in a fixed position rather than lower or raise it which appears to cause aggravation.

TREATMENT

1. CICUTA VIROSA 6c. This is a prominent remedy and is indicated by the lateral fixation of the head and neck to one side or the other. Abdominal symptoms such as vomiting may be present.

2. ACONITUM 6c. This remedy should if possible be given as soon as prodromal symptoms are noticed, e.g. the hypersensitivity to surroundings or undue awareness. Given at this stage subsequent involvement may be minimised.

3. STRAMONIUM 30c. When there is a tendency to fall to one side, invariably the left, this remedy may be found helpful. There may also be abdominal symptoms such as diarrhoea with a diminution in sight.

4. AGARICUS 6c. Staggering gait and progressive severity of symptoms may indicate the need for this remedy, e.g. slight sensitivity could lead on to furious attacks of mania or head-shaking.

5. BELLADONNA 30c. The indications for this remedy are convulsive fits accompanied by foaming at the mouth, throbbing pulses and redness of eyes. Pupils are markedly dilated and the animal feels hot all over.

FOOTNOTE. The reader will have noticed the similarity of the various remedies recommended and it is sometimes extremely difficult to determine which one to use. This task is not made any easier by the fact that the symptoms themselves have much in common. It will therefore be necessary in many cases to proceed on a trial and error basis.

2. DISEASES OF THE SPINAL CORD

These are relatively common and are related mainly to alterations in the spinal vertebrae and include injuries, disc disease and myelitis.

1. MYELITIS. This is the term used to denote inflammation of the substance of the spinal cord. It is occasionally met with and is due mainly to infective agents, e.g. the distemper virus.

CLINICAL SIGNS. Both motor and sensory nerve tracts may be involved giving rise to a variety of symptoms such as loss of sensation in the limbs and tail or paraplegia in those animals which are severely affected. Alteration to gait is not uncommon. There may also be loss of control over bladder and bowel functions.

TREATMENT. The following remedies have all been used with varying degrees of success and should give encouraging results in cases which are not too far advanced:

1. CONIUM MACULATUM 30c. This remedy is almost specific for animals which show hind-leg weakness ranging from slight ataxia to paraplegia where there is a progressive upwards involvement of the disease process.

2. LATHYRUS SATIVUS 30c. Indications for this remedy are paralyses of various kinds especially affecting the motor nerves and the remedy is relevant to other areas of the body besides the hind-limbs.

3. GELSEMIUM 30c. Mild cases showing a general weakness of the neuro-muscular system may benefit from this remedy. Smaller peripheral nerves are very often affected more than the larger nerve trunks, e.g. the nerves governing the throat and larynx.

4. CAUSTICUM 30c. A useful remedy for the older subject showing involvement of one particular nerve, e.g. the sciatic or the radial, giving rise to a localised paralysis. The subject which needs Causticum very often displays hard sessile warts on various parts.

5. SILICEA 30c. This remedy has a certain reputation in the treatment of spinal conditions of varying kinds and is worth considering if other overall symptoms agree.

6. ANGUSTURA VERA 30c. Paralysis of the legs and the joints of feet are commonly associated with this remedy.

2. INTERVERTEBRAL DISC DISEASE. Disc lesions occur when the cartilaginous disc itself loses its essential fluid, usually with age, and becomes fibrosed and eventually calcified. This can occur at an earlier stage in certain breeds particularly the Dachshund and Pekingese. Symptoms appear only when the disc protrudes from the intervertebral space and presses on the cord.

CLINICAL SIGNS. These depend very much on the degree of compression of the cord and the location of the lesion. Pain is a constant accompaniment of protrusion in the neck and lower back areas, while paraplegia is associated more with lesions in the thoracic and upper lumbar areas. Lesions in the cervical area result in a peculiar stumbling gait with the head outstretched and the neck muscles contracted. This causes great restriction of movement. If paraplegia occurs from lesions of the lower vertebrae, urinary incontinence invariably follows.

TREATMENT. The following remedies have proved their worth in practice:

1. *RUTA 6c.* This remedy has an extremely beneficial effect on injuries associated with bone and cartilage and gives good results in the treatment of vertebral complications.

2. *HYPERICUM 30c.* This remedy should be used in conjunction with the previous one. It has a specific action on nerve injuries and will quickly relieve the pain associated with spinal lesions, especially when these are more pronounced in the lower back or coccygeal area.

3. *HECLA LAVA 12c.* This remedy is indicated in those cases where calcification of the disc or discs is suspected. It has a reputation for limiting the degeneration process.

4. *CALC. FLUOR. 30c.* Indicated more in the earlier stages and will help regulate the calcium metabolism in a constitutional manner and thereby limit the scope of the trouble.

5. *SYMPHYTUM 30c.* Comfrey in homoeopathic form should be considered if injury is suspected as a contributory factor to the establishment of symptoms. It could usefully be combined with Arnica in this connection.

6. *ANGUSTURA VERA 30c.* This is a very useful remedy in conditions affecting the spinal cord and its use will limit any nerve damage which might ensue from disc protrusion. The neck of the animal gives the impression of heaviness because of an inability on the part of the patient to raise it effectively.

7. *CALC. CARB. 30c and CALC. PHOS. 30c.* Both these remedies will influence the calcium metabolism in the younger animal, the former for fat subjects and the latter more for the leaner subject.

FOOTNOTE. Injuries to the back which might involve the spinal cord as distinct from disc protrusion will benefit from one or other of the following remedies:

1. ARNICA. 30c. Should be considered as a routine remedy for all injuries and bruising where the skin is unbroken. It will limit the scope of subcutaneous haemorrhage and hasten resolution of blood clots and haematoma.

2. HYPERICUM 30c. This remedy is the main one for nerve injuries, especially where an open wound is present. The specific action on nerve endings will quickly relieve pain and promote healing.

3. LEDUM 30c. If the injury is of the punctured type, this is the remedy to be considered and can profitably be combined with the previous one.

3. ANKYLOSING SPONDYLITIS. This term refers to an inflammatory process of one or more vertebrae and is sometimes seen in old dogs. It leads to exostoses and arthritis of the vertebral joints.

CLINICAL SIGNS. Pain is evidenced in the early stages by arching of the back and there is usually paresis of the hindquarters later on but not usually paraplegia. It may be necessary to differentiate this condition from intervertebral disc disease by means of X-ray examination.

TREATMENT. One or other of the following remedies may give encouraging results if the disease process is not too far advanced:

1. RUTA 6c. This remedy has a beneficial action on the periosteum and will be found useful in the early inflammatory phase. It will prevent extension of the inflammatory process and thereby aid in the healing process. The tendency to arthritis should therefore be checked.

2. RHUS TOX. 6c. Early arthritic involvement will be helped by this remedy. The patient will show a disinclination to move but will improve if made to do so. Further extension of arthritis should be checked by its use.

3. HYPERICUM 30c. If nerves are involved in the inflammatory process, this remedy should be considered. It will quickly alleviate pain in this connection.

4. CONIUM MACULATUM 30c. Hind-leg paresis should be helped by this remedy and it gives the best results when used in ascending potencies.

5. CAUSTICUM 30c. This remedy also has a beneficial action on nerve weakness, more especially in the older subject and benefiting single nerves rather than any particular plexus.

Diseases of the Urinary System including the Bladder

These are of extremely common occurrence and are more frequently encountered in urban or built-up areas where the risk of spread from contagious diseases such as Leptospirosis is always present. It is normal to find a degree of kidney failure in the old dog, male animals being more disposed to this than females. The kidney conditions which concern us include Interstitial Nephritis, which is encountered in both acute and chronic forms, Pyelonephritis, Nephrosis and Urolithiasis or stone formation.

Other conditions less frequently met with are Hydronephrosis and Pyelitis. When we consider the bladder we find that cystitis is fairly widespread in both sexes, possibly more so in the female. The end result of any of these conditions (except cystitis) could be uraemia which can arise as a result of kidney failure when the kidney tissue is no longer capable of separating waste products and toxins from the blood.

1. INTERSTITIAL NEPHRITIS

(a) Acute Form This is probably the commonest kidney condition met with in the dog.

ETIOLOGY. Acute interstitial nephritis is invariably bacterial or viral in origin, the commonest cause being infection due to Leptospira species.

CLINICAL SIGNS. These can develop quite quickly and are at first accompanied by anorexia and depression. The patient exhibits increased thirst while vomiting is a fairly constant feature. A rise in temperature is seen in the early stages but may drop to near normal later. Signs of discomfort in the lumbar region are evident with tenderness over the kidney region and arching of the back. There is a disinclination to move and when the animal is encouraged to do so stiffness of movement is seen. The coat becomes dry due to dehydration while circulatory disturbance is shown by a full bounding pulse and discoloration of visible mucous membranes. Elimination of urine is decreased.

TREATMENT. There are many useful remedies employed in the treatment of this disease and these include the following:

1. ACONITUM 12x. This should always be given in the early stages if at all possible. At this stage the animal shows anxiety and distress and possibly fear. This remedy will do much to relieve the patient of these anxieties and help calm him.

2. APIS MEL. 200c. This is a most valuable remedy considering that changes in the kidney tissue are accompanied by oedema and swelling.

3. ARSEN. ALB. 1M. Indications for this remedy are the animals which show dehydration and harsh, dry coat accompanied by thirst for small quantities of water. The mucous membranes of the eyes are red and there may be vomiting and diarrhoea. Symptoms are usually worse towards midnight when the patient becomes increasingly restless.

4. BELLADONNA 200c. When this remedy is indicated the animal will feel extremely hot, with dilated pupils and a full bounding pulse. There are frequent attempts to pass urine which is scanty in amount and sometimes reddish-brown in colour. Signs of central nervous system involvement may be present, such as excitability and possibly a tendency to convulsions.

5. CANNABIS SATIVA 30c. There is a great desire to pass urine but little comes. The urine contains mucus and pus and possibly blood. Passage of urine is accompanied by pain evidenced by the animal crying out.

6. CHIMAPHILLA UMBELLATA 30c. Again there is scanty urine which is dark and contains sediment. Frequent desire is also present but symptoms are alleviated by the animal moving about.

7. BERBERIS VULG. 30c. Arching of the back and tenderness over the renal area are very pronounced when this remedy is to be considered. The animal prefers to stand and pains tend to move about over the whole lumbar area; all symptoms are worse on movement. The urine itself may be clear but often it is of a yellow colour indicating the involvement of the liver in the disease process.

8.   *TEREBINTHINAE 200c.* Symptoms of uneasiness disappear on movement. Frequent desire to urinate is present, the urine containing blood and smelling sweetly like turpentine or violets.

9.   *PHOSPHORUS 200c.* An important remedy which will help control vomiting which arises when liquids are rejected shortly after ingestion. There may be an accompanying gingivitis with small haemorrhages present when this remedy is indicated.

10.   *URTICA URENS 3x.* This remedy helps elimination of waste products via the urine and promotes urination.

The patient, being dehydrated, should have free access to water. Remedies such as *ARSEN. ALB.* and *PHOSPHORUS* should help control vomiting and also allow fluids to be retained. Homoeopathy has a decided advantage over conventional medicine in this respect when fluids have to be given intravenously to maintain an electrolyte balance.

(b)   Chronic Form. This is a progressive condition, varying degrees of which are found in the majority of dogs over eight years old, although clinical signs may not be present in all cases. There is no one outstanding cause and while degeneration of kidney tissue can follow the acute form and Leptospiral organisms are retained in the kidney it can also develop in the absence of any obvious existing factor.

CLINICAL SIGNS. Progressive loss of weight occurs which is accompanied by stomatitis, vomiting and increased thirst. The output of urine is increased, the urine itself being pale and watery. The specific gravity is low reflecting the retention of solids in the animal's tissues. Dehydration is a constant feature, the coat being harsh and dry while the skin may show scattered lesions of eczema.

TREATMENT. The following are the more prominent remedies to be considered:

1.   *ARSEN. ALB. 30c.* The remedy to be considered when the patient shows excessive dehydration with increased thirst and dry staring

coat. Itching of various areas may be pronounced and all symptoms are generally worse towards midnight.

2. *CHININUM SULPH. 6c.* The amount of urine passed is excessive when this remedy is indicated. The urine is pale and very watery, and may be strong-smelling. These symptoms are often accompanied by slight abdominal tympany which produces increased respiration. Skin rashes may be prominent.

3. *COLCHICUM 30c.* Again there is increased urination with frequency. The urine can vary from clear to dark-brown. There are usually accompanying joint pains indicated by stiffness and disinclination to move. Abdominal flatulence may be more extreme than that exhibited under the preceding remedy, and in addition ascites may be present.

4. *IODUM 30c.* A suitable remedy for the older patient and for those animals which show wasting accompanied by ravenous appetite. The coat is dry and superficial lymph glands may show hardness while diminishing in size. There may be frothy diarrhoea of a light creamy colour.

5. *MERC. CORR. 30c.* A useful remedy when the increase in urination is accompanied by straining with possibly mucous diarrhoea as well. Symptoms are worse in the period from sunset to sunrise. It appears to have a beneficial effect on the kidney tissue in general. Skin symptoms such as ulceration and red eczematous patches are frequently present.

6. *PHOSPHORUS 30c.* This remedy also has a beneficial or tonic effect on the kidney parenchyma. Output of urine is also increased and vomiting of stomach contents when they become warm is a strong guiding symptom for its use.

7. *PLUMBUM MET. 30c.* This remedy may be indicated in those conditions where excessive wasting over the lumbar region is accompanied by a tendency to paraplegia or weakness of the hind quarters. Other signs of incipient paralysis may arise such as difficulty in retaining saliva. Extreme constipation is invariably present.

8. *NATRUM MUR. 30c.* Excessive urination and frequency is a notable feature when this remedy may be needed, and this is often worse during the night. Mouth lesions in the form of superficial ulcers and blisters are often present while hawking and scraping of throat occurs.

2. PYELONEPHRITIS

This occurs more commonly in bitches and is frequently a sequel to cystitis and sometimes co-exists with it. It can arise when there is any obstruction to the passage of urine and leads to the presence of blood and pus in the urine. A specific bacterial cause is Corynebacteria renale, an organism which lodges in the kidney pelvis leading to the formation of purulent exudate. A secondary cystitis usually co-exists in this instance. Diagnosis is by the presence of purulent material and blood in the urine. The following remedies may help in cases not too far advanced:

1. HEPAR SULPH. 30c. This is one of the main remedies in combating pyogenic infections and treatment may have to be continued through various potencies to achieve results.

2. SILICEA 30c. Long-standing cases may respond to this remedy given over a period of two months giving a dose twice weekly.

3. MERC. CORR. 30c. Accompanying symptoms of slimy diarrhoea, salivation and skin ulceration may determine the use of this remedy. The urine frequently has a greenish tinge because of dissolved (characteristic) pus.

4. PAREIRA 6c. Severe straining with discharge of mucus from the urethra may indicate this remedy. There is extreme tenderness over the kidney region. The urine frequently smells strongly and there is severe difficulty in passing it, the animal assuming a pronounced crouching attitude.

5. UVA URSI 6c. With this remedy the urine is exceedingly slimy and contains whole blood and possesses a greenish tinge. Straining is again evident.

FOOTNOTE. It might be difficult for the owner or attendant to differentiate between these various remedies and in practice it may be necessary to try a different remedy if the most likely one fails to relieve. It should be possible to achieve relief of the condition from one or other of the above.

3. NEPHROSES

This is the term used to describe the degeneration and consequent necrosis of the secreting tubules of the kidney and their obstruction on account of various deposits within them.

ETIOLOGY. Various poisons and toxins are usually implicated, chief among which are chemical agents and secondary products from infected wounds or burns.

CLINICAL SIGNS. In the early stages there is marked diminuation of urine output and in severe cases when the secreting tubules are blocked with crystalline casts there may be a complete suppression of urination. The initial stage is shortly replaced by increased output of urine which shows blood cells and albumen casts.

Diagnosis of this condition depends very much on laboratory urine examination when specific gravity readings and other tests will reveal the exact nature of the problem.

TREATMENT. We have to rely mainly on remedies which have an action on the kidney parenchyma and have in addition the reputation of being good constitutional remedies. Chief among these are the following:

1. PLUMBUM MET. 30c. This metal in the crude state has a destructive action on kidney tissue and we should therefore expect it to have a beneficial effect in preventing further degeneration when used in potency. There may be an accompanying paraplegic tendency when it is indicated with the possibly peripheral nerve involvement as well.

2. PHOSPHORUS 30c. This element also has a necrotic and destructive effect on tissue such as kidney and liver, producing necrosis with accompanying constitutional signs such as vomiting and superficial haemorrhages.

3. SILICEA 30c. This remedy possesses the power of absorbing scar tissue which we would expect to be present in the kidney parenchyma when we consider the nature of the disease we are discussing. It could be of particular benefit to the naturally lean animal.

4. SOLIDAGO 6c. This is a useful remedy in the early dysuric stage, when the urine contains a thick sediment and is dark brownish-red in colour. The sediment may show a heavy phosphate content, and diarrhoea and/or dysentery may be present as well.

5. THUJA 6c. This is a good constitutional remedy in general. The urine is possibly frothy with cloudy sediment. The animal shows signs of pain by kicking or licking in the region of the bladder and the urine frequently dribbles away after the main stream has been passed.

6. *ARSEN. ALB. 30c.* Also a good constitutional remedy for the patient which shows dehydrated coat with diarrhoea, skin irritation and periodic vomiting. Symptoms are always worse towards midnight when the animal becomes increasingly restless and drinks frequently.

7. *MERC. CORR. 6c.* Animals with dry eczematous or ulcerated skins showing in addition slimy saliva and mucous diarrhoea may need this remedy. It has a marked action on the kidney parenchyma and is useful in higher potencies as well as lower.

8. *URTICA URENS 3x.* A useful remedy in the early dysuric stage when it may help produce diuresis. There is frequently an accompanying oedema of body tissues especially along the abdomen and chest. It possesses the ability of eliminating gravelly deposit from the tissues and produces a thick turbid urine.

4. UROLITHIASIS. Stone or Calculi Formation

This is a constitutional problem which has as its end product the formation and subsequent deposit in the renal pelvis and bladder of sabulous or gravel material which coalesces into stones or calculi. They are most commonly encountered in the bladder and occur more frequently in male animals.

ETIOLOGY OF CALCULUS FORMATION. Calculi which are predominantly made up of phosphates usually have their origin in an alkaline urine which can predispose to urinary infection. These are the most commonly encountered, others such as cystine or urate calculi occurring less frequently and more often in particular breeds because of genetic defects.

CLINICAL SIGNS. The first signs observed are usually the passage of blood and the presence of purulent material in the urine. Depending on the degree or advancement of stone formation there may be passage of thickened urine showing heavy deposits or more frank difficulty in passing urine. Pain in the bladder may cause the animal to cry out and lick or gnaw at the bladder area. Severe pain and discomfort attend the passage of urine which is usually voided drop by drop.

TREATMENT. Once large stones have formed the only rational treatment is surgical, but in the early stages when the sabulous material has not coalesced into calculi there are a number of useful remedies available which will prevent further deterioration and in some cases dissolve the gravelly material itself. Chief among these are the following:

1. LYCOPODIUM 30c. This remedy has a tonic action on the liver and will help control the metabolism of that gland, malfunction of which is frequently the cause of the tendency to gravel formation. Subjects which require it are frequently thin and wizened-looking showing reddish discoloration of urine on standing.

2. BERBERIS VULG. 6c. This remedy also acts in much the same way. Indications for its use include tenderness over the lumbar region with yellowish discoloration of urine.

3. HYDRANGEA 3x. This is an important remedy which helps both prevent calculi if given as a routine and also aids in the dissolution of sandy material making it easier to eliminate. The urine may contain white salts alternating with yellow sandy material.

4. EPIGEA REPENS 3x. Urinary deposits are of the uric acid type when this remedy is indicated. They take the form of a brownish deposit. There is much straining when attempting urination.

5. BENZOICUM ACIDUM 6c. This also has uric acid deposits in its provings but it differs from the previous remedy in giving the urine a disagreeable heavy odour. Catarrhal mucous sediment occurs.

6. THLASPI BURSALIS 6c. Phosphates are in abundance when this remedy is needed. It will quickly dissolve sabulous material and produce an increase in deposits of a brick-red colour when used in potency.

7. URTICA URENS. 3x. This remedy also thickens the urine and removes the tendency to gravel formation by removing the basic salts which help form it. It will also increase the quantity of urine passed.

8. CALC. PHOS. 30c. A good constitutional remedy which will regulate the Ca. and P. metabolism and so prevent the formation of phosphates. It should be given as a routine remedy in young animals up to the age of one year.

9. MAG. MUR. 6c. This remedy may have a part to play in preventing the formation of some forms of calculi and may be given like *CALC. PHOS.* as a routine remedy if the urine shows suspicious deposits and other signs of urolithiasis. It should thus be helpful in controlling the tendency to form more stones.

10. LITHIUM CARB. 6c. This remedy shows turbid urine containing a significant amount of mucus with dark-brown deposits. It aids liver function and helps control the tendency to manufacture more lithates.

11. OCIMUM CANUM 6c. This remedy is useful once gravel has formed. The urine is a bright-yellow colour with a musky odour. The sediment is brick-red in colour.

FOOTNOTE. As phosphates are the principal salts concerned in the formation of calculi in the dog, a diet which is on the acid side of ph will be of considerable help in preventing stone formation. This can be ensured by adding a teaspoonful of apple cider vinegar to the animal's food or drinking water daily. The dog may at first object to the taste but will soon adapt if the practice is persevered with.

5. CYSTITIS. Inflammation of the Urinary Bladder

This is a frequently-encountered problem which can affect dogs and bitches of all breeds.

ETIOLOGY. The cause is usually bacterial in the acute form but a significant number of cases may also be due to mechanical causes such as damage to the bladder lining due to the presence of calculi giving rise to a more chronic form. Streptococci, Staphylococci and forms of E. Coli are bacteria which have been implicated.

CLINICAL SIGNS. The principal sign is frequency of urination which is often attended by severe straining, the urine being voided drop by drop and usually containing blood. Constitutional upset is evidenced by fever with occasionally vomiting and diarrhoea. The animal resents pressure over the bladder region and the urine may be strong smelling and is usually dark in colour.

TREATMENT. The homoeopathic practitioner or attendant is fortunate in having at his disposal a plentiful supply of well proven remedies for the relief of this condition. Chief among these are the following:

1. ACONITUM 12x. Will be of value in the early feverish phase of the acute stage, helping to calm the patient and allay pain and fear.

2. CANTHARIS 6c. One of the principal remedies employed. The patient strains violently and passes blood-stained urine drop by drop, with great frequency.

3. CHIMAPHILIA UMBELLATA 6c Straining is again evident with this remedy but the urine passed contains more purulent material than blood. The urine is often dark-green and extremely strong. The patient appears to obtain relief by moving about.

4. COPAIVA 6c. The urine possesses a sweetish smell and has a frothy appearance. In the male animal there may be balanitis with attendant itching causing the animal to lick frequently at the affected parts. Frequent urging is also present.

5. CAMPHORA 6c. Urine is voided slowly and is of a yellow-green colour. On standing there occurs a reddish sediment. There may be retention of urine with ineffectual attempts at micturition.

6. EQUISETUM 6x. Frequent urination occurs but is not usually associated with straining. Passage of urine does not relieve symptoms of discomfort. Tenderness over bladder region extends towards the lower right flank. Frequency of urination is worse during the night.

7. EUPATORIUM PURPUREA 6c. A remedy which may relieve the more chronic form of cystitis due to the presence of calculi which leads to passage of a few drops of urine at a time. If such obstruction is removed by passing the stone, large quantities of urine may be passed, especially at night, the urine containing a high albumen content.

8. PAREIRA 6c. A useful remedy for the more chronic form in which the musculature of the bladder has probably become thickened and without tone. Urine continues to dribble away after the main stream has been passed. There is an odour of ammonia from the urine which is heavily contaminated with mucus.

9. CAUSTICUM 30c. A useful remedy in the recurrent or chronic form and is especially adapted to the older animal. It follows well after

CANTHARIS which may be needed if acute symptoms develop during a flare-up in the chronic form.

10.   SABAL SERRULATA 6c. A useful remedy more adapted to bitches than dogs as frequently there are accompanying ovarian or uterine symptoms. Tenesmus is present along with a glutinous mucus at the urethral meatus.

11.   TEREBINTHINAE 200c. Indications for this remedy include the presence of much blood in a scanty amount of urine. There is a sweetish smell from the urine resembling turpentine or violets. Symptoms of discomfort are eased by movement.

12.   UVA URSI 6c. Signs of pain or discomfort over the entire pubic area accompany the passage of greenish slimy urine containing blood and purulent material. There is straining and frequent attempts at passing urine which do not relieve symptoms of pain.

Diseases of the Cardio-Vascular System

1. THE HEART

Disturbances of the heart's function are extremely common in the dog as old age approaches and these take various forms depending on which part of the heart is involved.

Signs of Heart Disease. Apart from information which is obtained by means of the stethoscope (auscultation) and electrocardiogram examination, one of the main visible signs is generalised venous engorgement leading to oedema, especially ascites. Other signs such as dyspnoea and cough may also indicate heart disease although these can also occur in respiratory affections. Cyanosis of visible mucous membranes is a more useful guide. The 'heart cough' is a soft muffled sound somewhat like that produced as an accompaniment to distemper infection.

The pericardium, myocardium, endocardium and valves can all be affected but we will confine our remarks to the heart muscle and valves as these are much the more common structures to be affected.

1. MYOCARDIUM. Degenerative disease of the heart muscle sometimes occurs as a sequel to infectious disease and also to poisoning by certain metals. Hypertrophy of the muscle can also occur and this can be associated with kidney disease. Inflammation of the muscle — myocarditis — can occur as an accompaniment or sequel to infectious disease and is manifested by a fast weak pulse and signs of pulmonary congestion. Remedies which are useful in controlling this are *CRATAEGUS Ø or 1x* and *CONVALLARIA Ø or 1x. STROPHANTHUS Ø or 1x* has also proved useful. The diagnosis of myocarditis will be difficult for the layman and should properly be left to a clinician. Blood tests and electrocardiogram readings may be needed.

2. CONGESTIVE HEART DISEASE. This condition relates to an inability of the heart to supply sufficient blood to the tissues, thereby resulting in an overall sluggish circulation with the production of oedema in various areas, particularly the abdominal cavity (ascites). This in turn affects kidney function with an inability to excrete sufficient fluid in proportion to that formed.

ETIOLOGY. The main causes are congenital heart disease and acquired valvular disease, with lesions of the myocardium being a supplementary factor. The left (mitral) valve is the one usually at fault but generalised failure of function also occurs.

CLINICAL SIGNS. Ascites is the most commonly observed sign along with increased difficulty in breathing. Restlessness is a common feature, the dog frequently shifting position. The animal may assume a sitting posture to relieve pressure of abdominal fluid on the diaphragm.

TREATMENT. There are many useful heart remedies available, chief among which are the following:

1. LYCOPUS VIRGINICUS 3x. The pulse is quick and irregular. Breathlessness is pronounced.

2. ADONIS VER. 1x. One of the best remedies for valvular disease. Urine output is decreased and the urine contains albumen and casts. Heart action is rapid and feeble and oedema is pronounced.

3. CRATAEGUS Ø or 1x. This remedy will regulate the heart's action and show an accelerated pulse. Fainting turns may be present when this remedy is indicated.

4. CONVALLARIA 1x. The pulse is full and intermittent. Has an action somewhat similar to *LYCOPUS*. The animal is disinclined to take exercise.

5. LILIUM TIG. 6c. The pulse is small, rapid and weak which is made worse by even a slight movement. This is a remedy which may prove more suitable for bitches than dogs.

6. LAUROCERASUS 6c. Exercise may bring on extreme breathlessness with possibly fainting turns. Visible mucous membranes become cyanosed.

7. STROPHANTHUS 1x. This is a useful remedy for slowing the heart's action when there is a fast thready pulse. It will greatly strengthen the beat and will aid output of urine in ascites.

8. CACTUS GRANDIFLORUS 6c. Although the symptoms indicating the need for this remedy are mainly subjective it should be considered if other remedies fail to give the desired results, as it has frequently given good results in the treatment of many different heart conditions.

9. RUMEX 6x. This is a remedy which could prove useful in long-standing heart conditions in old animals. A dry spasmodic cough frequently accompanies breathlessness and hoarseness.

10. SPONGIA TOSTA 6c. This is also a useful remedy in chronic cases showing symptoms which are similar to the previous remedy but are much more severe. The respiration is violent and gasping.

11. CARBO VEG. 30c. This is a remedy which is extremely suitable for seemingly hopeless or moribund cases. It frequently restores deep breathing. It should be given in the evening when so-called asthmatic attacks supervene.

2. SHOCK

This term covers the condition which arises as a result of a decrease in the peripheral circulation and can arise from haemorrhage, extensive burning, sepsis and anaphylaxis (protein shock).

CLINICAL SIGNS. The animal becomes indifferent to its surroundings and appears unkempt. The eyes become sunken, body surface is cold and visible mucous membranes are pale. Increased respirations are the rule with occasionally large intakes of air. The pulse is weak and fast.

TREATMENT. The main remedy to consider is *ACONITUM 12c* which usually allays symptoms in a short time. *ARNICA 30c* and *CHINA 6c* are useful remedies if weakness and shock are a result of haemorrhage. *CARBO VEG. 30c* is useful in those cases showing air hunger and collapse.

FOOTNOTE. Dogs should not be artificially warmed when in shock and fluid may have to be given by injection in severe cases to combat disturbance to the circulation. The above remedies will materially aid these measures.

Diseases of the Muscles

1. MYOSITIS

Inflammation of muscle fibres is a well-documented syndrome in the dog, leading to degeneration of muscles in prolonged cases.

ETIOLOGY. The cause may be either systemic or traumatic. The loose description of 'rheumatism' being a cause is not really applicable to the dog. If the origin is systemic there is usually a bacterial infection present, while trauma is associated with injury of one kind or another.

CLINICAL SIGNS. There may be swelling of the particular muscle but frequently no special signs are evident and the owner's attention is drawn to the fact that the animal cries out on being moved or lifted. Various postures are assumed according to the muscles affected, e.g. arching of the back when the lumbar muscles are involved. A board-like feeling on the abdomen indicates pain of the muscles of that region.

TREATMENT

1. ACONITUM 6c. Should always be considered in the early stages and will bring about relief from pain, especially if the origin is bacterial. It will allay any tendency to shock if the condition arises very quickly.

2. RHUS TOX. 6c. This remedy is indicated when the animal gains relief from movement, even although the initial movement is painful. It may influence the muscles of the left side of the body more than the right, and could be indicated when severe wetting or prolonged damp is associated with the onset of symptoms.

3. BRYONIA 30c. Movement is resented when Bryonia is indicated. The animal will seek to lie on the affected muscles and pressure on them gives ease. Warmth is usually useful also.

4. CURARE 30c. Indicated when there is a generalised weakness or semi-paralysis of the muscles involved. Muscular reflexes are abolished.

5. *CAUSTICUM 30c*. This remedy is associated with an accompanying contraction of tendons and stiffness of muscles. Warmth gives relief. More adaptable to the older patient with unsteadiness of gait.

6. *ZINC. MET. 30c*. Associated with trembling of affected muscles which also show weakness. Usually arises from cases of systemic (bacterial) origin and may be indicated for a more general involvement of the neuro-muscular system.

7. *STRYCHNINUM 30c*. This remedy could be indicated when severe contractions of muscles take place as part of an overall systemic involvement. Various postures may be assumed.

8. *GELSEMIUM 30c*. Weakness and a tendency to paralysis is the keynote of this remedy. There may be a generalised involvement of all muscles and the trouble is usually systemic in origin. An attempt to exercise the animal can lead to collapse with severe fatigue.

2. MYOSITIS OF THE MASTICATORY MUSCLES

A specific form of myositis affects the German Shepherd breed or animals bred from them and occurs in both dogs and bitches. It is associated with an increase in certain white cells circulating in the blood and being deposited in the affected muscles. There is no known cause which can be regarded as exact.

CLINICAL SIGNS. The muscles of the cheek become puffed out, giving the face a pointed look and exerting pressure on the area around the eyes causing them to appear protruded. Pain is present in the early acute stage and the animal has difficulty in opening the mouth. Extension of the disease process to the throat results in tonsillitis and lymphadenitis. The inability to open the mouth results in progressive debility and weakness. Changes in the muscle fibres result eventually in fibrosis giving the muscles a hard sensation which accompanies the degeneration.

TREATMENT. This can be a difficult condition to treat but the following remedies are worth considering:

1. *CURARE 30c*. This remedy may help the function of the muscles and limit the tendency to paralysis.

2. *THUJA 6c.* This is a constitutional remedy which has given encouraging results in muscle conditions where hardening of fibres occurs and is reputed to have helped degenerative muscle conditions in other species.

3. *SILICEA 30c.* This remedy has a reputation for helping to limit the overproduction of white cells in certain pathological states and is therefore indicated indirectly in an attempt to limit the process.

4. *MERC. IOD. RUB. 30c.* This remedy has a specific action on the left side of the pharynx and may help inflammatory or other processes affecting this area including any neighbouring lymphadenitis.

5. *MERC. IOD. FLAV. 30c.* The same indications exist for this remedy but the right side of the pharyngeal area is involved.

6. *PHYTOLACCA 30c.* This is also a good general throat remedy and may help relieve any complications affecting this area.

3. MUSCULAR DYSTROPHY

This term covers a condition of degeneration of muscle with attendant atrophy and ultimately replacement of muscle strands with fibrous tissue. This eventually leads to an apparent increase in the muscle mass. The muscles chiefly involved are those of the hind-leg above the hock and those of the shoulder.

ETIOLOGY. Although a somewhat similar condition occurs in lambs and calves due to a shortage of Vitamin E in the metabolism of the growing muscle, this sequence of events has not been demonstrated in the dog in the natural state, although experimentation has produced it artificially. It may be due to an unknown hereditary factor affecting the metabolism of the muscles.

CLINICAL SIGNS. Progressive muscular weakness leads eventually to an inability to stand, preceded by varying degrees of paresis; a shuffling or stumbling gait ensues. Disease of the gastrocnemius muscle above the hock produces a 'dropped leg' appearance. Obesity is a frequent sign of systemic involvement.

TREATMENT. The addition of Vitamin E to the diet may help, especially if combined with the element Selenium. Remedies which should be used on a constitutional and symptomatic basis include the following:

1. *CURARE 30c.* General weakness and trembling of the affected muscles may show a response to this remedy.

2. *CALC. CARB. 30c.* This remedy may help the condition if it develops in young, fat or obese subjects. It will help regulate the general metabolism.

3. *SILICEA 30c.* Further degeneration of muscle fibres may be halted if this remedy is used early in the disease process. It has the power of dissolving scar tissue and removing any excess fibrosis.

4. *SELENIUM 30c.* Because of its Vitamin E content, this remedy should give good results as an adjunct along with other indicated remedies.

4. MUSCULAR CRAMP IN THE GREYHOUND

This condition, peculiar to this breed, affects animals when they are running and consists of a muscular spasm involving the hind-legs. Various theories have been advanced as to the cause, chief among which are fatigue and calcium deficiency. There is a superficial resemblance to azoturia in the horse but the condition in the dog is unaccompanied by the appearance of muscle pigment in the urine.

CLINICAL SIGNS. The animal quickly loses ground when racing or competing with others in training. Severe involvement leads to a dragging gait in which the dorsal aspect of the toes are unsupported and thus give a knuckling appearance when making contact with the ground. The lumbar muscles become tense and hard and the animal appears anxious and distressed.

TREATMENT

1. *ACONITUM 6c or 30c.* This remedy will quickly allay anxiety and help calm the animal.

2. ARNICA 30c. Should be given as a routine to help remove pain and allay shock.

3. RHUS TOX. 6c. Will help the sprain involved in any tendon involvement.

4. RUTA 6c. A useful remedy if periostitis has been produced by tearing of any ligament or tendon at its insertion.

5. BERBERIS VULG. 30c. This remedy will help relieve any lumbar weakness associated with radiating pains which could be present.

6. CURARE 30c. Should help relieve the stiffness of hind-leg muscles.

Diseases of the
Musculo-Skeletal System

1. BONE DISORDERS AND DISEASES

a) OSTEOPOROSIS. This term is used to describe the condition in which bone becomes increasingly porous. It is due to metabolic upsets which result in a deficiency of bone formation and may follow systemic disease of varying kinds. Exact diagnosis depends on X-ray examination. The animal may show an increased tendency to fractures.

TREATMENT. The following remedies may all prove useful:

1. CALC. PHOS. 30c. This is a very useful remedy for the younger animal in the growing stage as it exerts a profound influence on the development of bone and muscle. More suitable for lean animals.

2. CALC. CARB. 30c. This remedy has an action somewhat similar to the previous one but it suits the fat animal more than the lean one.

3. CALC. FLUOR. 30c. The fluoride of calcium is a good tissue remedy and is instrumental in hardening bone and strengthening the periosteum.

4. HECLA LAVA 12c or 1M. This remedy also exerts an action on bone producing in the crude state exostoses of varying kinds, excess of which leads to brittleness and fractures. Homoeopathically it gives good results in such cases.

5. SILICEA 30c. This is also a good tissue remedy exerting a beneficial action on the skeletal system in general.

b) MANDIBULAR PERIOSTITIS. This is a condition which is frequently seen in some small breeds, particularly the Scots Terrier and occasionally the West Highland White. Severe inflammation of the periosteum of the lower jaw occurs together with improper function of the mandibular-maxillary joint. It is thought to be hereditary.

CLINICAL SIGNS. These appear when the pup is approaching the age when the milk teeth are being shed and the permanent ones beginning to erupt. Pain is evident when the animal attempts to open the mouth and this refusal to eat is an early sign. The mouth is opened only with extreme difficulty. The lower jaw becomes grossly thickened especially near the mandibular-maxillary joint and there is an accompanying wasting of cheek muscle. Generalised weakness and loss of condition inevitably follow the inability to partake properly of food.

TREATMENT. The following remedies are worth considering:

1. HECLA LAVA 12c or 1M. This remedy exerts a definite action on the bone of the maxillary and mandibular areas. It will help resolve any exostoses and should help reduce the bony swellings.

2. CALC. FLUOR. 30c. More suitable for the milder or early case before bone thickening has become apparent. It is a valuable tissue remedy.

3. ACID. FLUOR. 30c. This remedy is a useful one if there are signs of bone necrosis evidenced by soft areas appearing along the maxilla or mandible. It is instrumental in regenerating bone.

4. PHOSPHORUS 30c. This element also exerts a beneficial action on necrosed tissue and could be useful in the early stages before serious changes have taken place.

5. RUTA 30c. This remedy could prove useful in the early stages where periostitis first sets in. It should therefore be given when the first signs of trouble appear.

6. SYMPHYTUM 200c. Homoeopathic comfrey may prove useful in averting the tendency to fracture which could arise as a result of rarefaction of bone.

c) OSTEOMYELITIS. This term refers to an infection of bone which, in the acute form, has its origin in the cavity of bone known as the medullary cavity. A more chronic form originates in the periosteum and leads to the formation of sinuses opening on the skin.

ETIOLOGY. The acute form arises when pyogenic bacteria gain entrance to the medulla of the bone either through blood transfer or via compound fractures. Chronic osteomyelitis can develop when infections reach the periosteum and can follow punctured wounds or bites. The main pyogenic organisms which are associated with this disease are Staphylococci and to a lesser extent Streptococci.

CLINICAL SIGNS. Acute disease is characterised by lameness, febrile attacks and swelling of the affected limb. Sinus formation with purulent discharge is often the early sign of the chronic form, and febrile signs are much less evident. X-ray examination is advised in doubtful cases.

TREATMENT. The following remedies are useful in controlling both the acute and chronic forms:

1. ACONITUM 30c. Should always be given in the early febrile stage of the acute stage. It may have to be repeated for one or two doses.

2. HEPAR SULPH. 30c. In the acute form accompanying severe pain this could prove a very useful remedy. A guiding symptom for its use is extreme sensitivity to pain.

3. RUTA 6c. This remedy has a beneficial action on infections or inflammations of the periosteum and should therefore prove beneficial in the acute form which may thus prevent the more chronic form arising.

4. CALC. PHOS. 30c and CALC. CARB. 30c. These two remedies could prove useful in treatment of the young animal in the developing stage.

5. SILICEA 30c. A suitable remedy for the chronic form where sinuses have formed.

6. TUB. BOV. 30c. Although this condition is not thought to be associated with tuberculosis as it is in the human being, it is nevertheless worth keeping in mind as a useful remedy in controlling bone affections of this nature.

7. SYMPHYTUM 200c. This remedy should help allay the tendency to any weakening of bone structure and is generally a good healing agent.

8. STAPHYLOCOCCUS AUREUS 30c. Should be combined with selected remedies, one dose usually being sufficient.

d) RICKETS AND OSTEOMALACIA. These terms denote a failure of bone to assimilate minerals such as calcium and phosphorus, leading to softening of bones and distortion and thickening of joints. The term 'rickets' is used to describe the condition on the young growing animal, while the other relates to the same condition in the adult animal.

ETIOLOGY. The basic cause is failure of the calcium and phosphorus metabolism and is related to a deficiency of Vitamin D.

CLINICAL SIGNS. The softening of the bones in rickets produces a 'bandy-legged' appearance, while enlargement of the joints at the end of the bones leads to painful swellings. These appear as bead-like protuberances when the ribs are involved. Early involvement produces severe lameness. Osteomalacia is less associated with bone distortion and lameness is the predominant symptom. X-ray examination will confirm suspected cases.

TREATMENT

1. Rickets. The main remedies to be considered are *CALC. CARB.* and *CALC. PHOS.* both used in 30c potency. The former is suited to fat puppies while the latter acts better in the leaner animal. Both of these remedies greatly assist the calcium metabolism.

2. Osteomalacia. *SILICEA 30c*, *HECLA LAVA 12c* and *ACID. PHOS. 30c* are all useful remedies in helping to strengthen bone formation. Twice-weekly doses for eight weeks should prove beneficial.

e) OSTEODYSTROPHY. OSTEODYSTROPHY FIBROSA. In the dog this condition is often associated with kidney disease and leads to softening of the bone and a failure of new bone to become mineralised. The classifications above refer to the older animal and the younger respectively.

ETIOLOGY. Interstitial nephritis and pylonephritis have both been implicated in the causation of this condition. The impaired renal function results in excess elimination of calcium, phosphorus and potassium with the result that the body seeks to recover these by calling on the skeletal reserves. The parathyroid glands also play a part by being involved in calcium metabolism.

CLINICAL SIGNS. The flat bones are more at risk than the long ones and the bones of the face and head are particularly affected. Signs of kidney disease will be obvious (see chapter on Diseases of the Urinary System). Weakness and loss of appetite are present indicating systemic upset while signs of anaemia are evident in paleness of visible mucous membranes. Increased intake and output of water is a frequent accompaniment. Bones fracture easily. Blood examination and X-rays may be necessary in doubtful cases to establish a true diagnosis.

TREATMENT. One or other of the following remedies should provide some degree of relief:

1. CALC. FLUOR. 30c. A good general tissue remedy which has a favourable action on bone development.

2. CALC. PHOS. 30c and *CALC. CARB. 30c* will aid the condition in the young animal.

3. RUTA 30c. A useful remedy for the initial inflammatory involvement of the periosteum of bone.

4. ARSEN. ALB. 30c or *1M.* This remedy may be indicated in those cases showing anaemia and general weakness.

5. HECLA LAVA 12c. A good remedy which should help prevent fracture of bones.

FOOTNOTE. One or other of the remedies listed in the chapter on Diseases of the Urinary System may be needed depending on whether or not overt signs of nephritis are present.

Diseases of the Blood
and Blood-Forming Organs

1. ANAEMIA

This is the general term given to a diminution in the amount of haemoglobin in the blood. Haemoglobin is the vehicle which transports oxygen in the red cells and any reduction in its circulation causes weakness with pallor of visible mucous membranes. Anaemia can arise as a direct result of loss of blood which could be due to a sudden haemorrhage or to slow bleeding which may be present over a longer period of time. Parasite infestations and some infections also give rise to anaemia while disease of bone-marrow may produce the condition by interfering with the production of blood cells.

a) ANAEMIA DUE TO ACUTE HAEMORRHAGE. This invariably corrects itself if not too severe and the blood-forming organs soon make good the loss of red cells. Remedies which will hasten the coagulation of blood and reduce bleeding include the following, all of which have been well proven:

1. ACONITUM 12x. For any acute tensive state leading to congestion with fever or inflammation. Such conditions could cause rupture of superficial blood vessels, e.g. in the nose leading to epistaxis. Blood usually bright red.

2. ARNICA 30c. When haemorrhage is due to the effects of trauma or extreme congestion. Bleeding may take place from any orifice and is due to stasis giving rise to passive haemorrhage of an oozing nature. Blood may be dark.

3. FICUS RELIGIOSA 6c. A good anti-haemorrhage remedy. Vomiting of blood may take place, also from uterus and bowels.

4. MILLEFOLIUM 30c. Blood is bright-red and frequently associated with acute conditions showing a rise in temperature. The urine may contain blood and haemorrhages also occur from lungs and bowels.

5. CROTALUS HORR. 200c. Haemorrhages are frequently associated with septic states and jaundice but not always. The blood is dark and remains fluid, coagulation frequently being entirely lost. There is a general tendency to haemorrhage throughout the body and the urine becomes dark red.

6. *VIPERA 6c.* Like other snake venoms, this particular one causes passive bleeding with an additional neurotoxic action. Haemorrhages are often related to the area of lymphatic vessels.

7. *LACHESIS 30c.* This remedy again is associated with conditions which bear a similarity to those brought about by snake bite. In the particular case of Lachesis there is an accompanying bluish or purplish discoloration of skin and haemorrhages are dark and passive. Septic involvement is again a feature.

8. *IPECAC. 30c.* Haemorrhages are profuse and gushing with the blood bright-red. Has proved a very effective remedy in post-partum bleeding, the blood coming in large gushes instead of a steady stream. There may be an associated vomiting and loathing of food. Bleeding may also occur from the bowel and the lungs.

9. *MELILOTUS 6c.* A very useful remedy for nose-bleed of bright-red character. The blood vessels of the neck and throat are tense and throbbing. There is a general tendency to congestion of the arterial system.

10. *HAMAMELIS 30c.* This is a useful remedy for controlling haemorrhages associated with passive congestion of the venous system. Nasal bleeding is common and also haemorrhages from the uterus and lung.

b) ANAEMIA ASSOCIATED WITH MALFUNCTION OF THE HAEMOPOIETIC SYSTEM. Bone marrow dysfunction which produces pernicious anaemia in man is not observed in the dog and such malfunction in this species is referred to as aplastic anaemia. It is usually associated with toxins or severe infections of a chronic nature, e.g. it has been known to arise as a result of over-prescribing with certain powerful drugs.

It may also be associated with vitamin deficiency and it is good practice to administer organic vitamin supplements to the dog as a routine measure. Among the more important of these are Vit. E and those of the B complex.

CLINICAL SIGNS. These are similar to those of anaemia in general.

TREATMENT. The remedies listed under 'anaemia' are also applicable in this connection but in addition the following remedies should be considered:

1. TRINITROTOLUENE 30c. There may be an accompanying toxic jaundice present when this remedy is indicated. It is an extremely useful remedy in restoring the power of the haemoglobin to transport oxygen. There are also present weak heart-beats and highly-coloured urine.

2. SILICEA 200c. This is a remedy to consider if it is thought that the condition has arisen as a result of long-standing infections. It is a valuable remedy also if the anaemia accompanies general malnutrition and it has a specific action on bones in general.

3. ARSEN. ALB. 1M. This deeply-acting remedy will aid those cases showing extreme weakness and exhaustion with accompanying restlessness and thirst for small amounts of water. It has a valuable reputation in chronic anaemia.

4. MERC. SOL. 30c. Mercury produces severe anaemia and is a remedy which should be considered when the specific accompanying symptoms are present, e.g. Ptyalism and slimy diarrhoea with skin eruptions.

c) HAEMOLYTIC ANAEMIA. This is the term given to that condition which arises as a result of severe intravascular destruction of red blood cells, the bone marrow being unable to produce enough cells to compensate for the loss.

ETIOLOGY. In canine practice it is usually associated with invasion by protozoa or bacteria and also perhaps to chronic lead or other metallic poisoning. Among the more common agents are Babesia canis (a protozoan organism) and Clostridium welchii and Streptococci of varying kinds among bacterial agents.

CLINICAL SIGNS. There are the classic indications of anaemia in general but there may also be seen specific weaknesses affecting abdominal and leg muscles which become tender to the touch. In severe cases the animal may be so weak that it is unable to rise, and visible mucous membranes lose their colour completely. The haemoglobin which is released by the destruction of the red cells gains entrance to the circulating blood stream and appears in the urine giving the latter a reddish-brown appearance and in severe cases a more general 'port wine' colour. Jaundice is invariably present.

TREATMENT. Those remedies listed under the two previous headings will also be appropriate in this connection but in addition *CINCHONA 30c* (China) should be added to restore strength to the patient after loss of body fluid.

GENERAL NOTES ON ANAEMIA. In all cases of suspected anaemia, the animal's blood should be subjected to a proper laboratory examination. This will determine the type of anaemia present and whether there is in addition a corresponding imbalance in the leucocyte (white cell) count which could indicate some accompanying disorder.

Diseases of the Joints

Included under this heading are conditions which produce inflammatory changes, viz. arthritis, and those which cause deposition of new bone — arthropathies. It is common practice, however, to use the term arthritis in the broad sense to cover all joint inflammations and degenerative changes.

1. ARTHRITIS DUE TO INFECTION

This is brought about by the introduction to the joint of pyogenic bacteria chiefly by injury, the main organisms being Streptococci and Staphylococci.

CLINICAL SIGNS. There is an initial temperature rise and febrile signs develop. The affected joint becomes swollen, tense and hot. Pain is obvious by the onset of severe lameness. Examination may reveal the presence of punctures on the skin and the appearance of a purulent exudate. This latter must be differentiated from synovial fluid, escape of which can occur if the wound has penetrated the joint capsule. This fluid has an oily feel and is less opaque than purulent exudate.

TREATMENT
1. ACONITUM 30c. This should be given as soon as possible in the early febrile stage if noticed in time.
2. FERRUM PHOS. 6c. This also is a good remedy for the initial feverish stage, more often indicated when throat symptoms accompany the invasive process.
3. BELLADONNA 30c. Indicated when the patient presents an excitable picture with dilated pupils, throbbing arteries and a hot skin.
4. BRYONIA 6c. The indications for the use of this remedy are a deterioration of symptoms on movement, relief from pain on pressure over the joint and a possible involvement of the respiratory tract. The joint is usually extremely hard and tense.

5. *APIS MEL. 6c*. If the synovial sheath of the joint becomes oedematous, indicated by soft fluctuatory swellings, this remedy may help. The patient is made worse by heat in any form, and is invariably thirstless.

6. *LEDUM 6c*. This is the remedy of choice if the arthritis has been caused by the initial penetration of a sharp object giving rise to a punctured wound.

7. *IODUM 6c*. This is a remedy which sometimes gives good results in the less acute case, especially when joint pains are worse at night. When this remedy is indicated the patient is often thin with a voracious appetite and the skin is dry and withered-looking.

8. *RHUS TOX. 6c*. The indications for this remedy are relief from movement, although there may be an initial stiffness on rising. There may be accompanying skin symptoms of a vesicular, itchy nature.

9. *SILICEA 30c*. This remedy is indicated in the more chronic case. There may be involvement of neighbouring lymphatic glands showing cold abscesses.

The intercurrent use of Streptococcal and Staphylococcal nosodes is also indicated.

2. SIMPLE ARTHRITIS. So called Rheumatoid Arthritis

True rheumatoid arthritis as it occurs in man is thought not to occur in the dog and the syndrome in this species, which goes by the popular description, is a polyarthritis of systemic origin affecting mainly older animals particularly of the larger breeds.

CLINICAL SIGNS. Lameness is first evident and there is increasing difficulty in rising as the condition progresses. The joints are normal-looking in the early stages but become larger as the disease develops due mainly to deposition of new bone (osteoarthritis). Skin lesions accompanying these changes have also been noted. The animal may improve on exercise and show a response to differing weather conditions.

TREATMENT. The following remedies may give some measure of relief in the early stages and have given encouraging results:

1. RHUS TOX. 6c. One of the main indications for the use of this remedy is relief of symptoms on movement. The patient may be stiff and disinclined to move but once exercise is taken symptoms appear to be less pronounced. A deterioration is often seen in wet or damp weather and skin symptoms in the form of vesicular rashes sometimes accompany the condition.

2. BRYONIA 6c. This remedy is indicated when the patient appears better at rest, exercise or movement tending to aggravate. The joints appear tense and may be hot and swollen indicating an accompanying synovitis.

3. ACID. SALICYLICUM. 6c. Indicated especially when the smaller joints such as the carpus and metacarpal region are involved. Movement aggravates, while the application of dry heat relieves the symptoms. All affected joints are tender on touch.

4. IODUM 6c. This is a useful remedy in chronic states and may be indicated when the patient is lean with dry, staring coat and a tendency to exhibit voracious appetite, and glandular swellings, which later may tend towards atrophy. Joint pains increase during the night, and are made worse by touch or pressure. Dropsical swellings of the joints may occur leading on to suppuration.

5. CALC. FLUOR. 30c. When this remedy is indicated there are usually cracking noises in the joints and there is a tendency to dislocations. Synovial membranes are also involved, giving rise to swellings. Bony deposits (exostoses) may also arise.

6. ACTAEA RAC. 6c. There may be a generalised involvement of all joints when this remedy is needed, especially those of the lower vertebrae and around the hip joint, associated muscles become involved.

7. CAULOPHYLLUM 6c. The smaller joints are chiefly affected, particularly those of the feet and cervical vertebrae. It could be the remedy of choice in bitches which have a history of genital disturbances of one kind or another.

8. LITHIUM CARB. 6c. The joints of the hind limbs are more involved than the fore. There is difficulty in ascending stairs. The hip joints may show alternate involvement.

9. OSTEOARTHRITIC NOSODE 30c. This nosode has been developed from joint-fluid in affected cases and has been used with success either by itself or in conjunction with appropriate remedies.

3. ANKYLOSING SPONDYLITIS

This condition is not uncommon in the dog and is confined to the vertebral column. There is a breed disposition, prominent among sufferers being representatives of the Dachshund, Great Dane and Boxer breeds.

ETIOLOGY. The exact cause has not been determined with accuracy but it appears to follow protrusion of an intervertebral disc because of inflammatory degeneration of the ligaments supporting it. This is followed by ankylosing of the vertebral joint.

CLINICAL SIGNS. Acute pain accompanies the early lesions. The animal's movements become unsteady and paraplegia or paresis ensues, according to the severity of the condition. Arching of the back is a common feature. There may be urinary incontinence. Doubtful cases can be confirmed or rejected by X-ray examination.

TREATMENT. The following remedies may all give good results if treatment is started early in the pathological process:

1. RUTA 6c. This remedy has a specific beneficial action on the periosteum of bone and will limit the early inflammatory process, especially that surrounding the sacro-iliac region.

2. HYPERICUM 30c. This is one of the main remedies for the relief of pain because of its selective action on injured nerves. It acts especially well in combination with the preceding remedy in the treatment of the condition under discussion. The lower end of the back from the sacrum to the coccyx is particularly affected.

3. CALC. CARB. 30c. Indicated in fat subjects, e.g. mainly in the Boxer and similar types. Attacks may come on suddenly, and give rise to cramping movements which precede joint involvement. It will help regulate the calcium metabolism and reduce the tendency for calcium to be deposited in joints.

4. CALC. FLUOR. 30c. A tendency to dislocation is common and there may be other joints affected besides the vertebrae.

5. HECLA LAVA 12c. This remedy has a selective action on bone and used homoeopathically will aid those cases where exostoses appear because of deposition of new bone.

4. OSTEOARTHRITIS

This is the term used to describe degenerative joint-disease where the articular cartilages become eroded and bony exostoses occur at the margin of the joints. The hip and stifle joints are the ones most commonly affected.

ETIOLOGY. Although age undoubtedly plays a large part in the onset of these changes, systemic or metabolic disturbances are also involved. Progressive mild inflammation in the joint over a period of time is more likely to produce osteoarthritis than any other predisposing factor. Obese and heavy animals may develop it more readily than lighter dogs. Poor conformation also contributes. Once the cartilage degenerates the cushioning effect is lost within the joint and the joint capsule then becomes progressively involved.

CLINICAL SIGNS. Lameness is the principal sign and may involve several joints. Unwillingness to use the affected limb or limbs results in muscular wasting. Later signs include thickening of the joint. The worst affected limb may be held in a flexed manner.

TREATMENT. This is not an easy condition to treat satisfactorily and the earlier it is started the more likely it is that deterioration will be slowed down. Among the more useful remedies for the early inflammatory stages are the following:

1. RHUS TOX. 6c. This remedy is indicated when the animal's symptoms are eased after movement progresses for a short time. There may be initial stiffness on first moving.

2. BRYONIA 6c. The indications for this remedy are the opposite of the preceding, viz. the animal prefers to remain still and any movement causes distress and sometimes acute pain evidenced by the animal crying out.

3. *ACTAEA RAC. 6c.* This may be needed if accompanying muscles are involved as indicated by a heaviness in the limbs and the animal appearing to be generally stiff and cumbersome when trying to move.

4. *CAULOPHYLLUM 6c.* This remedy could well be indicated if the condition is confined to the smaller joints, e.g. carpus, tarsus and the joints of the toes.

5. *LITHIUM CARB. 6c.* With this remedy the smaller joints are also more prone to involvement. Application of warmth eases the pain. Small nodular swellings may be felt in the joints.

6. *CALC. FLUOR. 30c.* May be needed in the later stages once exostoses and joint swellings develop. The carpus is the main joint affected when this remedy is indicated. There may be accompanying cystic tumours around the joint.

7. *HECLA LAVA 12c.* This is another useful remedy when exostoses have developed and will help limit the deposition of new bone.

5. BURSITIS

By this term we mean the appearance of a swelling over the joint, those particularly affected being the points of the elbow and the hock.

ETIOLOGY. Damage to the bursa of the joint due to overweight is a common contributory factor as is also irritation of the part by repeated contact with the ground if the animal is inclined to rest more than is usual.

CLINICAL SIGNS. The acute form shows swelling, heat and pain, evidenced by lameness. Effusion into the bursa occurs and this accounts in part for the increase in size. When bursitis is chronic, fibrotic changes take place leading to the formation of a solid lump in the affected area. This may eventually ulcerate leading to secondary infection.

TREATMENT

1. *APIS MEL. 30c.* This is a useful remedy in the early inflammatory state where effusion is taking place and the joint is extremely tender to the touch. The animal may lick and gnaw at the joint because of itching irritation. The patient shows an intolerance of heat and touch.

2. *BRYONIA 6c.* Indicated when the joint is enlarged and pressure over the area brings relief as also does the application of cold compresses. The animal resents movement and prefers to lie on the affected joint.

3. *RHUS TOX. 6c.* If surrounding ligaments and tendons are involved to any great extent, this remedy may be needed. Movement 'limbers up' the animal which is in need of Rhus Tox.

4. *IODUM. 6c.* This remedy may be needed if the affected animal is lean with excessive appetite and dry, lustreless coat. The joint capsule may be involved causing a general joint enlargement.

5. *CALC. FLUOR. 30c.* This is a good general tissue remedy and has a beneficial effect on the development of cysts, cystic tumours and fibrous swellings.

6. *SILICEA 30c.* This is another good 'long term' remedy which will help dissolve any associated scar or fibrous tissue. It will be beneficial if surface ulceration occurs leading to secondary infection.

Affections of the Skin

GENERAL CONSIDERATIONS

Skin affections of the dog fall into one or other of the following categories:—

1. External affections of parasitic origin, e.g. mange, ringworm.
2. Affections due to the presence of hyperplastic tissue, e.g. those originating from tumours.
3. Affections not due to physical agents, e.g. burns.

The skin performs essential functions such as excretion (e.g. of toxins), temperature regulation, and secretion (e.g. from sebaceous glands). It also forms a protective cover. There may be an increase (hyperaesthesia) or an absence (anaesthesia) of skin sensation, while many skin ailments are accompanied by severe or mild pruritus which may or may not be associated with systemic disease. Itching, which may take the form of gnawing, scratching or biting, is responsible for the development of secondary infection, pyogenic bacteria gaining entrance to the subcutaneous tissues once the skin is broken. As in other disturbances of health, when treating skin diseases homoeopathic medication must be directed towards the patient as a whole, and if possible the dog's constitutional remedy should be sought and given prior to treatment with an associated remedy. The constitutional remedy is not easy to elicit in all cases, but occasionally a remedy 'stands out' as it were, and we are able to recognise the type accurately, e.g. the Mercury, Pulsatilla or Sulphur type. Close examination of all symptoms and discussion with the owner as regards habits and modalities will usually narrow the choice of remedy, and enable a proper prescription to be made.

NUTRITION. If the intake of proper food is inadequate, this will be reflected in the quality and appearance of the coat, e.g. a harsh, dry coat may arise accompanied by the shedding of superficial epidermal cells (dandruff). Excess or deficiency of vitamins and an imbalance of the carbohydrate, fat and protein ratio can also cause disturbances of the skin.

PROTEIN. Essential for the production of amino-acids, this basic material is the normal food requirement of the adult dog, although the addition of a little fat and vegetable matter is also essential. Puppies require different amounts as well as different types of protein, e.g. they can assimilate more muscle meat than the adult dog, while the latter should have several small meals rather than one or two large ones as this encourages better assimilation and utilisation of food. Protein intake should constitute about a quarter of the total diet and may take the form of ordinary meat or fish together with milk.

FAT. This should be given in the form of unsaturated fatty acid, e.g. in a good vegetable oil (sunflower and safflower having the highest percentage of unsaturated fat). Deficiency of fat intake may lead to alopecia in puppies, preceded by dryness of the hair. Older dogs also show loss of hair together with redness of skin. If fat deficiency is of long standing, certain recognisable skin lesions arise. These include thickening of tissue over the paws and around the metacarpal joints. Ear discharges have also been known to occur, excoriating the ear flap, while temperamental changes may take place, e.g. excitability and peripheral muscle tremors. Essential fat requirement may be ensured by the addition of a teaspoonful of a suitable vegetable oil to the daily diet. Of these sunflower seed oil is probably the best.

CARBOHYDRATE. Requirements of this factor should be given in the form of grain products or root vegetables such as parsnip, beet or carrot.

VITAMINS. These are essential and are normally present in a balanced diet, but it may be necessary to supplement Vitamin E. Fresh liver is a rich source of Vitamin B12 and should be included in the diet twice weekly. Skin conditions which may arise because of lack or deficiency of vitamins are: hyperkeratosis, swelling of eyelids, susceptibility to infections (Vitamin A), severe itching, necrosis, threatened gangrene (Vitamin E), de-pigmentation of hair (Vitamin B factor).

MINERALS. Essential trace elements are present in a normal diet. Puppies will require calcium and phosphorus in the correct proportion, viz. one of calcium to two of phosphorus. These minerals should be administered in the form of *CALC. PHOS.*, as young dogs will utilise them better in this way. Magnesium deficiency may cause redness of the skin and affections of tendons. It should be given as *MAG. PHOS.* Iodine deficiency is associated with dry coat, poor growth of hair and anaemia. It should be used in the form of *KALI HYDRIODICUM*. Iron, sodium and potassium are also essential minerals. Lack of iron may cause localised oedema with paleness of skin, while dryness and ulcerations may arise in the absence or deficiency of salt. Pregnancy and lactation will impose demands on the brood bitch and her skin may suffer if her diet is not adjusted accordingly, e.g. there should be an increased intake of minerals and vitamins while maintaining her proper requirements of other factors. Lactation will demand adequate calcium and phosphorus. In puppies fed on cow's milk the addition of *MAG. CARB.* to the milk will be beneficial.

When studying the nutritional requirements, consideration should be given to the following points:

1. The amount of food taken in may not be enough due to, e.g. simple lack of appetite or other factors such as alimentary or other disease.
2. The presence of worms may affect absorption of the proper amount of food as may also the effects of drugs on the intestinal mucous membrane.
3. Dysfunction of the liver or pancreas may interfere with the proper utilisation of food after absorption.
4. Excess secretion of certain glands and diseases such as nephritis and diabetes may interfere with utilisation. So also could diarrhoea.
5. Animals undergoing regular severe exercise may require increased intake of food and water, e.g. racing greyhounds, hunting dogs.

ALLERGIC SKIN DISEASES

These occur frequently in the dog and take the form of dermatoses of various kinds. They are more often encountered in the summer, although neglected or badly-treated cases may show chronic symptoms all the year round.

ETIOLOGY. Skin allergies may have their origin in external factors, e.g. sensitisation of epidermis, or be due to toxic factors from within.

CLINICAL SIGNS. Generalised itching is present in most cases and may be more severe when the skin becomes exposed to warmth or be aggravated by cold conditions. The skin itself may show slight to moderate redness without any other changes, or become thickened and be accompanied by a degree of alopecia. The abdomen and inner thighs particularly show an erythematous and papular rash.

Eczemas of various types can be considered under this heading, although not all forms of eczema are allergic in origin. They may be acute or chronic, wet or dry with clinical signs and symptoms more or less in keeping with those outlined above. Severe pruritus may cause secondary infection due to pyogenic bacteria and is evidenced by suppurative lesions.

TREATMENT. According to symptoms and modalities displayed, the following remedies will help. There is a vast range of remedies applicable to skin conditions, but only the more commonly used can be mentioned.

1.   SULPHUR 30c or 200c. Indicated when the skin is red and itching is intense, made worse by heat. The gums may be unduly red. Papular or vesicular rash may also be present. It is a good intercurrent remedy and may be given with other remedies to enhance their action or at the beginning of treatment generally.

2.   ARSEN. ALB. 30c to 1M. When the skin is dry and scaly, shedding of epidermal scales occurring and accompanied by harsh, lustreless hair. The animal seeks warmth and shows a desire for small quantities of water frequently taken. Symptoms become worse after midnight and systemic disturbances include diarrhoea of cadaverous odour.

3.   RHUS TOX. 6c to 1M. This remedy should be considered when the skin symptoms are aggravated by wet and the dog shows stiffness when moving after rest but moves more easily when exercise proceeds. The skin shows papular or vesicular rash with much itching and redness. Warmth lessens the severity of the symptoms.

4. ANTIMONIUM CRUD. 6c. When skin lesions are more pronounced on the neck, back and limbs, taking the form of papular eruptions which later become scabby, discharging a yellowish secretion. Itching is worse towards evening and aggravated by warmth.

5. MEZEREUM 6c. Useful when skin lesions appear on the head, taking the form of large scabs with an underlying purulent discharge. There is a sensitivity to touch. Itching rash is common over bony areas the rash being surrounded by a red zone. The condition tends to be exacerbated by scratching and warmth. Should be considered in chronic eczema where symptoms agree.

6. HYPERICUM 1M. This is a suitable remedy for sensitisation due to external factors, e.g. photosensitisation. The resulting skin lesions may affect non-pigmented areas and appear as reddish ulcerated areas which itch and have a peeled look. There may be accompaning systemic changes such as jaundice.

7. HEPAR SULPH. 200c. The remedy of choice when lesions show extreme sensitivity to external stimuli and pus is beginning to form. The skin is usually swollen and shiny with a tense appearance. It is helpful in drying up the underlying purulent discharge in those cases attended by crusts and scabs.

8. PSORINUM 1M. This nosode may be necessary in eczemas of a particularly unpleasant nature with pronounced musty odour and severe itching. The skin is usually dry, and the lesion is frequently of a vesciular or pustular type.

9. BACILLINUM 200c. As a general inter-current remedy which activates the skin, this nosode will be of service. It is particularly suitable in cases with dry scaly lesions.

10. TELLURIUM 30c. When this remedy is indicated the skin lesions usually take the form of circular reddish areas, frequently on both sides of the body in symmetrical fashion. The outer ear flap is a predilection site.

SKIN CONDITIONS DUE TO EXTERNAL FACTORS

1. FOLLICULAR MANGE. This form of mange attacks young animals, e.g. under one year, although the effects may be noticed at a later stage. Two main types of this condition exist:— 1. Squamous,

2. Pustular, depending on the ages of skin attacked, while the type of skin also plays a part.

ETIOLOGY. The mite Demodex folliculorum is the cause and there is a predisposition to the disease congenitally.

CLINICAL SIGNS
a) Squamous Type. The hair follicles are attacked by the mite which also inhabits the neighbouring sebaceous glands. The hair soon falls out giving a bald appearance generally over a wide area of skin, although smaller areas may also be affected. Corrugation of the skin is the outcome together with dryness and scaliness while a bluish discoloration develops over the bare patches. Pruritus is generally absent.

b) Pustular Type. In this form the hair follicles become the seat of small pustules most often seen around the mouth, outer elbow and hock and in the axillary region. Extension of lesions leads to the development of small fistulae which secrete pustular material.

TREATMENT
a) Squamous Type. This should be instituted at the first sign before permanent damage can be done. There are excellent topical applications available nowadays which are very effective, but their use will be enhanced by the administration of the following remedies according to symptoms and stage of the disease:

1. SULPHUR 30c. A good general remedy which alters the conditions favourable to the development of the mite. Dose: one twice daily for a week.

2. KALI ARSEN. 30c. Suitable for more advanced cases which begin to show corrugation of skin. The animal may be restless and seek warmth. Dose: one daily for five days.

3. LYCOPODIUM 1M. This remedy will help stimulate growth of hair provided the disease is not too advanced and destruction of hair follicles has taken place. Dose: one daily for one week.

b) Pustular Type
1. HEPAR SULPH. 30c. Possesses a powerful action on purulent infections of hair follicles. In this potency will abort the pustular process. Dose: one daily for one week.

2. *KALI ARSEN. 30c.* As for squamous type.

3. *SILICEA 30c.* A useful remedy for those cases showing extension of lesions into fistulae. Dose: one daily for five days.

4. *CALC. SULPH. 6x.* This is also a useful remedy for healing pustular lesions, with small yellowish scabs. Dose: one three times daily for three days.

5. *MEZEREUM 6c.* A remedy which is more useful when the lesions are chiefly on the head or face. Small scabs coalesce and cover purulent areas. Dose: one twice daily for one week.

6. *THALLIUM ACETAS 30c.* Thallium in potency possesses the power of obviating the effects of trophic lesions on the skin and subcutaneous tissues. It thus encourages growth of hair on denuded areas and is a suitable long term remedy in both forms of mange. Dose: one twice weekly for one month.

2. SARCOPTIC MANGE. This form of mange is much commoner than the follicular type and although less frequently encountered nowadays it is occasionally seen in animals kept in overcrowded, unhygienic conditions.

ETIOLOGY. The parasite is an acarus called Sarcoptes scabei and is allied to the human scabies mite.

CLINICAL SIGNS. Unlike follicular mange this form is attended by severe irritation, biting and licking on account of the intolerable itching which is set up. This is made worse by warmth and the animal seeks cool places whenever possible. The disease is extremely contagious and frequently more than one dog in a pack or kennels is affected. Predilection sites are the base of the tail, the outer ear flap, around the eyes and on the forelegs, although any part of the body may be attacked giving rise to bare patches as a result of the hair having been bitten or scratched out. Handling the animal produces a reflex scratching movement. The affected areas show numerous small pimples which soon become scabby. A heavy musty odour is characteristic while in prolonged or untreated cases the skin becomes thickened and develops a folded appearance.

TREATMENT. Modern dressings are suitable and again should be supplemented by the following remedies which will hasten cure and prevent re-infestation:

1. SULPHUR 30c, 1M and 10M. This is the most important remedy and should be given in these ascending potencies, one dose of each on three consecutive days.

2. ARSEN. ALB. 1M. For animals which drink frequently, are restless and experience an aggravation of symptoms after midnight. There may be an associated diarrhoea of cavaderous odour while unaffected areas of skin are dry and scaly. This remedy could profitably be employed after *SULPHUR* because of its beneficial effect on the skin generally. Dose: one daily for one week.

3. HYDROCOTYLE 30c. This remedy could be of use in more advanced cases where corrugation and thickening of the skin has taken place. It also has a beneficial action on the small pustules which arise. Dose: one twice daily for one week.

4. PSORINUM 1M. Occasionally an animal will be met with where *SULPHUR* has failed to produce a completely satisfactory response. When this happens Psorinum will probably bring about the desired result. Dose: one daily for three days.

5. SEPIA 30c. Gives good results constitutionally when given as a convalescent remedy after the administration of the foregoing remedies. Dose: one per week for four weeks.

PREVENTION. When mange appears in a kennels or boarding establishment *PSORINUM* should be given to all in-contact dogs. This remedy, being the scabies nosode, can be employed prophylactically as well as therapeutically. One dose daily for three consecutive days.

3. OTODECTIC MANGE. Although more often encountered in the cat, it is also seen in the dog and leads to irritation of the affected areas.

ETIOLOGY. A specific mite is responsible.

CLINICAL SIGNS. The attention of the owner is first directed towards the animal shaking its head and rubbing the ears with its paws. On examination of the ear, excess brownish wax is evident which usually contains the specific parasite. The skin behind the ear flap may become excoriated due to scratching and resembles an eczematous lesion.

TREATMENT. After thorough cleansing of the ear with a mild solution of e.g. hydrogen peroxide, the following remedies should be considered:

1.   HEPAR SULPH. 6x. This remedy will allay internal inflammation of the ear canal which leads to the production of wax. Dose: one three times daily for four days.

2.   MERC. CORR. 30c. This will also help allay inflammation of a more severe nature especially if purulent infection supervenes. Dose: one daily for five days.

3.   TELLURIUM 30c. A useful remedy for allaying inflammation of skin behind the ear flap and for controlling the tendency to otitis externa. Dose: one twice daily for one week.

4.   SULPHUR 30c. Two daily doses will act constitutionally and make the animal less susceptible to infestation. It will also aid the action of other remedies and may be given concurrently.

4. RINGWORM. This skin condition affects mainly the younger dog and may be related to the general health of the individual, e.g. those whose resistance to disease is below normal are more liable to contract it.

ETIOLOGY. There are two main groups of ringworm fungi which attack dogs:—

1. Microsporum.
2. Trichophyton.

CLINICAL SIGNS

1. Microsporum Infestation. There is a natural affinity with the hair and initial infection soon leads to adjacent hair follicles becoming involved, causing secondary changes such as a crusty appearance and possibly a vesicular eruption. The areas most commonly affected are the head, neck and legs, lesions developing into circular areas which coalesce with neighbouring ones to produce widespread involvement in severe cases. Pruritus is common in the early stages. The lesions develop a crusty feel and sometimes these are not obvious, e.g. in long-coated breeds. Occasionally lesions may be seen around the claws.

2. Trichophyton Form. This fungus produces lesions about half an inch in diamaeter which take the form of raised scabs with a darker pitted centre. Any lesion may become the seat of secondary infection by pyogenic bacteria.

TREATMENT. The following remedies will be helpful in hastening resolution when combined with any suitable fungicidal dressing:

1. BACILLINUM 200c. This nosode has frequently been used successfully without recourse to any external dressing. Dose: two doses at two weekly interval.

2. KALI ARSEN. 30c. For the early pruritic stage. More suitable for the restless animal which shows aggravation of symptoms after midnight, and thirst for small quantities of water. Dose: one daily for five days.

3. CHRYSAROBINUM 6c. When the disease has progressed to the crusty stage with confluence of affected areas. Scaly eruptions are common around the eyes and ears. Dose: one three times daily for five days.

4. TELLURIUM 30c. This remedy has proved useful in skin ailments where lesions take a circular formation (as in ringworm) and also a tendency to equal distribution on either side of the body. Dose: one twice daily for one week.

5. SEPIA 1M. A suitable remedy where lesions take the form of small separate nodules with little tendency to coalesce. Dose: one twice weekly for two weeks.

5. ACUTE BACTERIAL DERMATITIS. This is a specific inflammation of the epidermis.

ETIOLOGY. Various organisms may be implicated but the common-est are members of the Staphylococcal and Streptococcal families, frequently producing a mixed infection.

CLINICAL SIGNS. The initial lesion takes the form of a vesicular rash, the vesicles coalescing to form a raw area which exudes serum. Severe irritation is set up causing the animal to lick the area more or less constantly producing extension of the original lesions. Purulent material is soon evident because of secondary infection.

TREATMENT. The affected areas should be washed clean with warm water containing Calendula and Hypericum lotion, the quantity being added in a strength of 1/10. The following remedies should be considered:

1. SULPHUR 6c or 30c. This remedy should always be given first as it helps clear the blood of impurities which could add to the general inflammatory state.

2. RHUS TOX. 1M. Useful for the initial vesicular stage with erythematous swelling. Severe itching is present causing the vesicles to rupture and produce a reddened area. Scratching does not relieve. There may be associated symptoms suggesting rheumatism such as difficulty in rising but symptoms generally alleviated by movement, the animal showing consistent restlessness.

3. ANTIMONIUM CRUD. 6c. When this remedy is indicated, lesions are seen more often on the upper parts of the body and are worse in the evening. The vesicles have a nettle-rash appearance and may appear like measles, discharging a blood-stained exudate. Itching is intense and the symptoms are worse by warmth and from touch. Signs of alimentary disturbance may be seen, such as disinclination to eat with vomition.

4. BORAX 6c. For erysipelatous inflammation with lesions appearing around the buccal area and on the lower limbs. The vesicles are pale and surrounded by a red zone. Salivation may be present. There is a tendency to early suppuration.

5. COMBINED STAPHYLOCOCCUS and STREPTOCOCCUS NOSODES 30c. The intercurrent use of these nosodes will materially aid the action of the other remedies, and they could also be used curatively by themselves in mild cases.

6. CHRONIC BACTERIAL DERMATITIS. Furunculosis. This is of more frequent occurrence than the acute form, large breeds of dogs being especially susceptible.

ETIOLOGY. Staphylococci and Streptococci are again implicated but the former more commonly.

CLINICAL SIGNS. Selected areas of infection occur around the feet, hock, elbow and occasionally the mouth, taking the form of puffy swellings with the overlying skin assuming a polished appearance. The skin soon ulcerates discharging a blood-stained fluid from numerous sinuses. Again the animal licks the lesions frequently because of irritation, extending its borders. This leads eventually to thickening of the skin which is gathered into folds. A 'proud-flesh' appearance is not uncommon while secondary infection by pyrogenic bacterial leads to a purulent discharge.

TREATMENT. According to the stage of the disease the following remedies should prove useful:

1.   RHUS TOX. 1M. For the early swelling particularly if associated with reddening of skin which looks erythematous, and for lesions around the hock and elbow. There is usually severe itching causing licking and scratching.

2.   SILICEA 30c. This remedy is the ideal one for the stage of ulceration with discharging sinuses particularly when these become purulent. Especially suitable for the leaner breeds and for lesions on the feet. Pus which forms is usually thin and grey. This remedy acts well in dogs with light-coloured coats.

3.   HEPAR SULPH. 6x. When the lesion is attended by extreme sensitivity to touch and the discharge is thin and blood-stained before pus has actually formed. It is applicable to lesions in any area but particularly those around the mouth. It will also produce good results in the later purulent stages when the pus is yellowish and blood-stained. In low potencies (e.g. 3x to 6x) it will promote suppuration and clearing of sinuses, while in higher potencies (e.g. 200c to 1M) it will abort the suppurative process and promote resolution.

4.   CALC. SULPH. 6c. Has a somewhat similar action to *HEPAR* but has not the same sensitivity to external factors. Its use is restricted to the stage when pus has formed and has little or no action earlier. More suitable for lesions on the limbs.

5.   TARENTULA CUB. 6c. When the original swelling is hard and extremely painful with a surrounding red zone. When ulceration occurs the sinuses are seen to run into one another, producing a central crater full of blood-stained material and pus. There may be systematic feverish symptoms.

7. NOCARDIOSIS. This is a bacterial condition which usually assumes the form of a granuloma which sometimes becomes suppurating. It may affect underlying tissues as well as the skin.

ETIOLOGY. Various species of nocardia have been associated with this condition.

CLINICAL SIGNS. Although these granulomatous swellings appear on the skin, they are in reality subcutaneous in origin. They may appear anywhere but favourite sites are the neck, chest and flank. The granuloma takes the form of a firm tumour-like mass which slowly grows in size accompanied by a degree of pain. Some forms show extreme sensitivity. As the disease progresses, ulceration takes place and pus is discharged from underlying sinuses. Secondary spread takes place including involvement of neighbouring lymph glands which, however, seldom show suppuration. Occasionally the animal exhibits feverish symptoms.

TREATMENT

1. FERRUM PHOS. 6x. This remedy may be of use in the early stages of development when it acts by reducing hyperaemia at the site of the lesion. This in turn serves to limit growth. It is mainly a right-sided medicine and granulomata may favour the right neck and shoulder areas.

2. HEPAR SULPH. 6x to 200c. The principal remedy to be considered when pus is starting to form although not yet visible. The main keynote of the remedy is extreme sensitivity to pain or external stimuli. When given in high potency it will abort the suppurative process while its employment at lower strengths will promote the expulsion of purulent material.

3. SILICEA 30c. A useful remedy for the ulcerative stage when sinuses have formed and pus is discharging. More suitable for the chronic case which keeps on breaking out. The quality of the pus is thin and greyish in colour. It will also help to remove scar tissue from healed areas and hasten resolution of the granulomatous mass.

4. CALC. FLUOR. 30c. When the neighbouring lymphatic glands become involved this remedy should help. The glands are usually of stony hardness and usually painless. This remedy will also have a beneficial effect on the size of the granuloma.

5. PYROGENIUM 1M. If feverish symptoms develop in severe cases with threatened collapse and septicaemic complications. The guiding symptom for the use of this remedy is a variation in the temperature to pulse ratio, e.g. a high temperature associated with a weak thready pulse.

OTITIS EXTERNA, including EAR CANKER and OTORRHOEA (see also chapter on the Ear)

Under this heading are included all forms of external ear trouble with or without discharges, irrespective of causation.

ETIOLOGY. The majority of cases are constitutional in origin and should be looked on as specific types of eczema. Some are associated with ear mites, the action of which is accentuated in breeds with long ear flaps, occluding the free passage of air.

CLINICAL SIGNS. The attention of the owner is first drawn to the animal shaking its head or pawing and scratching at the ear. Frequently the ear is rubbed on the ground. One or both ears may be affected but not usually to the same extent. On examination, the skin inside the ear flap is inflamed and possibly ulcerated due to scratching. Discharge may or may not be present, but if it is it is usually thin and acrid at first, becoming purulent later. A characteristic musty heavy smell accompanies this manifestation. Occasionally eczematous patches appear on the outside of the ear flap close to the head. Prolonged affections lead to thickening of the ear flap, with an inability to raise the ear properly.

TREATMENT. If discharge is copious, the ear should be gently syringed with a 1/10 solution of *CALENDULA* and consideration given to one or other of the following medicines:

111

1. *SULPHUR 30c*. If noticed in the early stages when the ear flap shows a reddish inflammation. There may be accompanying red areas around the anus and above the tail. The preliminary use of this remedy will also aid the action of other remedies in more advanced cases.

2. *RHUS TOX. 6c*. When this remedy is indicated, the ear flap is also reddened and inflamed but in addition numerous small vesicles are usually present. Itching is intense. Systemic symptoms may be present in the form of stiff joints which are eased by exercise.

3. *ARSEN. IOD. 6c*. The left ear is more often affected. The inflammation is accompanied by a thin serous acrid discharge which corrodes the skin. There may be coryza with an aggravation of general symptoms towards midnight. The animal is restless and drinks small amounts frequently.

4. *MERC. CORR. 30c*. When the discharge takes the form of greenish purulent material accompanied by the characteristic heavy smell. There may be an accompanying diarrhoea or dysentery, and the ear flap usually shows thickening. The purulent discharge may be seen from the nose also.

5. *HEPAR SULPH. 30c*. Indicated when the inflammation renders the ear extremely sensitive to touch. The neighbouring lymphatic glands are usually swollen and tender. There may be purulent discharge which will tend to dry under the influence of this potency.

6. *PULSATILLA 30c*. This is a suitable remedy for timid, affectionate dogs showing bland catarrhal discharge with swelling of the ear flap. Symptoms are worse in the evening and hearing is diminished.

7. *TELLURIUM 30c*. Eczematous lesions appear on the outer ear flap when this remedy is indicated. The left ear is more often affected and produces an acrid watery discharge with offensive smell. Neglected forms may show ulceration of the tympanum with suppurative discharge.

ALOPECIA

Falling out of hair is usually constitutional in origin and may follow systemic disease or be due to hormone dysfunction.

CLINICAL SIGNS. The sides and lower back areas are chiefly affected and in severe cases the skin may be rendered completely hairless, assuming a black polished appearance. Pruritis is generally absent except perhaps in cases associated with eczema.

TREATMENT. If constitutional disease is suspected this should be tackled according to symptoms shown, while those cases dependent on hormone imbalance should be given the appropriate hormone. Homoeopathic remedies which may help include the following:

1. LYCOPODIUM 1M. Systemic conditions which may indicate the need for this remedy include liver dysfunction shown as jaundice, and aggravation of general symptoms between 4 and 8 p.m. Early greying of the hair, e.g. around the muzzle, may be seen.

2. SEPIA 1M. More suitable for bitches especially if the loss of hair follows parturition. There may be an accompanying uterine discharge.

3. PIX LIQUIDA 6c. This remedy may help when the skin has a cracked look instead of the more commonly encountered polished appearance. Bronchial symptoms such as coughing up purulent sputum could also be present.

4. KALI ARSEN. 30c. This is a good general skin tonic and will greatly strengthen the hair and encourage growth.

5. USTILAGO MAYDIS 30C. When patchy alopecia affects the head. The lesions are usually circular and show no tendency to coalesce.

6. THYROID 1x. Hormonal deficiency is usually related to the thyroid gland and a low potency like this given for a few weeks should be sufficient to stimulate hair growth.

7. THALLIUM ACETAS 30c. Because of its action on skin and epidermis where it produces trophic lesions, this remedy in potency should be given as long-term therapy over a period of 3 to 4 months at infrequent intervals.

INTERDIGITAL ECZEMA — INTERDIGITAL CYSTS

This common condition is included under diseases of the skin as the great majority of cases are constitutional in origin and constitute a specific form of eczema.

CLINICAL SIGNS. The dog licks its paw frequently and in severe cases lameness is evident. Examination of early cases reveals a reddish area between two toes, sometimes extending up the leg a short distance. Progression of the trouble leads to the development of a small pea-like nodule which may be hard or soft and sometimes filled with dark blood. Some forms are less tender than others but the majority of cases are attended by extreme sensitivity. Neglected cysts show a tendency to extend in the form of sinuses or fistulous tracts with purulent exudation.

TREATMENT. According to the type of cyst one is dealing with the following remedies are indicated:

1. HEPAR SULPH 6c to 30c. This is the remedy of choice in the early stages and also for established cases where the chief guiding symptom is extreme sensitivity. If there is a tendency to pus formation the lower potencies will promote a free drainage while high potencies will abort the suppurative process.

2. SILICEA 30c. For hard cysts of longer duration than those needing *HEPAR.* Also indicated for fistulous tracts and sinuses showing thin greyish pus. This remedy has the power of rapidly healing such lesions and absorbing any attendant scar tissue.

3. GRAPHITES 6x. A suitable remedy for the softer cyst filled with dark blood. The surrounding skin is greasy and may secrete a honey-coloured exudate while numerous cracks may appear in the area and on the pads.

4. CALC. SULPH. 6c. Suitable for young dogs with excessive weight and poorly-nourished tissues. It is indicated once pus has formed and has found an outlet, healing taking place with attendant greenish scabs.

5. SECALE 6c. If neglected cases are encountered where the part has a necrosed and withered look and gangrene of the area is threatened, this remedy will promote healthy circulation and healing.

URTICARIA

By this term is meant the production of small weals or plaques under the skin and accompanied by a degree of itching.

ETIOLOGY. There are various causes, some constitutional, others external. Puppies may experience it due to faulty feeding or at teething, while change of environment may bring it about, e.g. a boxer dog was severely affected when on a seaside holiday from an industrial town.

CLINICAL SIGNS. The plaques may appear on any area and show as soft fluctuating swellings filled with fluid. The head and limbs are particularly affected and the former may show extensive oedema. Urticaria due to external causes such as contact with stinging nettles produces a similar picture.

TREATMENT. The following remedies should be considered:

1. APIS MEL. 30c. The most effective remedy for the diffuse oedematous form caused by coalescence of neighbouring plaques. The lesions may be hot or cold and the plaques or oedematous areas show pitting on pressure.

2. CALC. CARB. 30c. A suitable remedy for young fat puppies with defective assimilation, and a tendency to rickets.

3. CHAMOMILLA 6c. If dentition in the young dog is thought to be a contributory factor, this is the remedy to be considered. There may be an accompanying greenish diarrhoea.

4. NUX VOM. 6c. If thought to be due to faulty feeding and subsequent indigestion. Constipation may be present.

5. URTICA URENS 6c. The main remedy for urticarial weals dependent on external allergic causes, although it may also be used for cases not dependent on these. It will promote urination and so lessen the fluid content of the oedematous plaques.

6. ACONITUM 6c. Should always be given as a preliminary remedy, especially in cases of sudden onset.

7. RHUS TOX. 6c. If there is an accompanying cellulitis with redness of skin and severe itching, this remedy will be found useful.

WARTS

Although these manifest themselves on the skin, they are invariably systemic in origin.

ETIOLOGY. Many warts are due to viruses, but some are constitutional, dependent on disorders of metabolism.

CLINICAL TYPES. Warts vary greatly in character. Some are flat and sessile, firmly adherent to the skin. Others are pedunculated, thin and long. They may be smooth, corrugated or jagged-looking and may bleed easily on touch. Common sites for their occurrence include the eyelids, ears, head and upper chest. In the older animal the wart assumes a cauliflower-like appearance and is found principally on the head, particularly the nose, and the limbs.

TREATMENT. This varies according to the type of wart.

1. THUJA 6c. The chief remedy for pedunculated warts, although sessile types are also susceptible to its action. They are usually tender to the touch and bleed readily. It may be necessary to continue treatment with a higher potency, while the external application of tincture will materially aid the internal action of the remedy.

2. ACID. NIT. 30c. For cauliflower-like warts associated with a generally unhealthy skin which ulcerates easily and tends to discoloration. Lesions are frequently encountered around orifices, e.g. warts may surround the mouth, eyes and anus or vulva.

3. CALC. CARB. 30c. Small smooth warts are usually associated with this remedy, found on most areas and more often encountered in puppies, especially if flabby and overweight. The skin itself is usually flaccid and rough and may show accompanying eruptions of a pimply nature.

4. CAUSTICUM 6c. For rough-coated warts seen especially on chest and lower limbs. The skin surrounding the warts is usually inflamed and painful. There may be associated respiratory distress such as hard dry coughing. More often indicated for the older dog.

5. SABINA 6c. This is a lesser-used remedy but has been used successfully in bitches which have developed wart-like growths as a sequel to whelping associated with post-partum haemorrhage. The warty growths are dark and mole-like in appearance.

6. DULCAMARA 30c. For wart-like growths which develop from pustular inflammation, especially on lower limbs. The skin generally may have a scabby inflamed look, while lesions commonly appear when cool evenings follow suddenly after warm days, e.g. in Autumn. Also the animal is generally worse in wet weather.

Diseases of the
Female Reproductive System

The bitch is monoestrus and normally comes into season twice a year, roughly in spring and again in the autumn. The 'season' lasts about 17 days and can be divided into four stages:

1. Absence of heat in the normally healthy bitch, a condition referred to as **anoestrus**. This stage lasts from the very early changes up to the beginning of the next stage as follows:—

2. **Proestrus**. This stage lasts about nine days and is the period of preparation in which the Graafian follicle is growing and leads to accumulation of follicular fluid. The material contains a steroid hormone — oestradiol, which along with other substances known as oestrol and oestriol constitutes oestrogen. This stage is associated with vulval bleeding.

3. **Oestrus**. The stage of heat proper when the bitch shows excitement and desire and in which the ovary has matured along with the Graafian follicle. During this period the bitch will normally accept the male. It lasts on the average nine to ten days but occasionally a few days longer. Ovulation takes place during this time.

4. **Metoestrus**. This follows the regression of oestrus and extends to about 12 weeks. Early in this stage the follicle ruptures and the ovum is expelled. The follicular cavity is filled by the embryonic corpus luteum. This body secretes progesterone, the function of which is to prepare the endometrium or womb lining for the implantation of the fertilised ovum. At the same time oestrogen is inhibited and maturation of other follicles suppressed. It also controls mammary development.

The disease or abnormalities which concern us relate to the ovaries and the uterus. Breeding problems as such will be dealt with under a separate heading.

1. THE OVARIES

Inflammation of the ovary is referred to as ovaritis and is not normally a condition of importance in the bitch. If present it may be suspected by the animal gnawing at the flank or flanks and stretching out the hind legs. There may be a vaginal discharge. Symptoms are very much subjective in this condition, but remedies which have a selective action on the ovary include the following and are worth considering if ovarian trouble is thought to be present.

1.   APIS MEL. 30c. As acute inflammation is usually attended by a degree of oedema, this remedy may help in this connection.

2.   PULSATILLA 30c. This remedy will suit the affectionate bitch which exhibits changeable behaviour and sometimes shows a creamy uterine discharge.

3.   PALLADIUM 6c. The right ovary is more commonly affected when this remedy is indicated and symptoms extend upwards involving the peritoneum.

4.   PLATINA 6c. Suitable for highly-strung and excitable animals which show no disposition to be unduly friendly. Signs of abdominal pain in the pelvic region are often pronounced.

5.   LACHESIS 30c. Should be considered if left ovarian trouble is suspected. The skin is often bluish-purple in colour when this remedy is indicated, particularly over the mammary area, and in addition throat swellings may be prominent.

6.   CIMICIFUGA 30c. The bitch exhibits tenderness over the pelvic area which is worse in the lower left area. There is usually an accompanying muscular weakness and stiffness.

7.   IODUM 30c. A suitable remedy for the lean animal with dry coat and exhibiting abnormal appetite. Superficial lymph glands are small and hard and mammary tissue becomes thin and shrunken. The urine assumes a dark yellowish green colour.

2. DISEASES OF THE VAGINA AND VULVA

Apart from surgical conditions such as tumour formation and hyperplasia and prolapse of the vagina, which do not concern us here, the common condition is an inflammation of the vulva and vagina, both frequently being present together.

VULVO/VAGINITIS. Signs of this condition include redness and swelling accompanied by oedema. Examination of the mucous membrane reveals the presence of small red nodules on the vaginal wall. A clear discharge may be present and in neglected cases this may become purulent. The bitch will probably be seen licking the vulva while straining is evident after the passage of urine.

TREATMENT. The following remedies are all useful according to symptoms:

1. ACID. NIT. 30c. This is a valuable remedy where inflammation affects the mucous membrane near body orifices with or without ulceration. Discharge may be haemorrhagic. There is sometimes an accompanying diarrhoea of a slimy nature.

2. ANTIMONIUM CRUD. 6c. The parts are excessively itchy and a uterine discharge of a creamy nature is usually present. Skin eruptions of a pimply nature may accompany the condition.

3. APIS MEL. 30c. Will help to control the oedematous swelling and remove the stinging pains which are usually present. This remedy should be given as early as possible when swelling is first noticed.

4. RHUS TOX. 6c. The vaginal mucous membrane is intensely red and itching and swelling is severe. Constitutional upsets such as blistery skin eruptions may be present, together with stiffness of movement which decreases with exercise.

5. CANTHARIS 6c. Indicated when there is severe straining during and after the passage of urine. The bitch may exhibit frenzied sexual behaviour. Itching of the genital area is intense.

6. HELONIAS 30c. Fever, itching and swelling are associated with this remedy, together with sacral weakness which produces a dragging movement on attempting to rise. Catarrhal exudation is usually present.

7. KREOSOTUM 30c. Ulceration of vaginal mucous membrane accompanies an acrid, dirty discharge. Itching is intense. There may be superficial haemorrhages affecting skin and gums.

3. THE UTERUS

METRITIS or Inflammation of the Womb

This takes the form of acute and chronic disease:

a) ACUTE METRITIS. This is invariably associated with the parturition complex and runs a short course of up to five days.

ETIOLOGY. Chief among the causes of this condition is retained placenta together with infection which gains entrance to the genital tract as a result of faulty obstetrical procedure, e.g. lack of asepsis.

CLINICAL SIGNS. There is an initial rise in temperature and the bitch is obviously uneasy and lethargic. There may be diarrhoea and vomiting along with signs of dehydration. The eyes are sunken and have an anxious expression. Thirst is increased but the appetite remains poor or absent. Uterine discharges are present and vary in character from muco-purulent in mild cases to dark-brown containing blood-stained material in the more severe form.

TREATMENT. This should be instituted as soon as premonitory signs appear after parturition which has resulted in dead pups and difficult labour.

1. ACONITUM 30c. Should be given at once when it will quickly allay shock, fear and anxiety and regulate the circulation.

2. BELLADONNA 30c. Indicated when the animal is hot to the touch, with a full bounding pulse and dilated pupils. Signs of cerebral excitement may be present with, in extreme cases, convulsions.

3. APIS MEL. 30c. Also useful in the early stages when a degree of oedema will be present in the uterine lining.

4. LILIUM TIG. 30c. A good general remedy for uterine congestion leading to blood-stained discharges and straining in the pelvic region.

5. PYROGEN 1M. One of the most valuable remedies in this condition when the animal is almost comatose with a high temperature and a weak thready pulse. It is usually indicated following a septic metritis resulting from retention of dead foetuses or placentae. All discharges are extremely offensive.

6. *SABINA 6c.* A useful remedy following retention of placenta or when a bright red haemorrhage is present. This could occur after miscarriage when this remedy is probably most useful.

7. *SECALE 6c.* Haemorrhages are also present when this remedy is to be considered but in this instance the blood is fluid and dark. The patient is cadaverous-looking with cold extremities which are deficient in blood supply.

8. *ECHINACEA 3x.* This is another valuable remedy, very useful in puerperal complications. There is generally an accompanying septicaemia with offensive discharges. The abdomen exhibits a threatened peritonitis, being hard and tympanitic.

b) **CHRONIC METRITIS**. Signs of this form are usually noticeable only at parturition when the pups are born dead or die soon after birth. If this has been known to occur, the most rational treatment is to have the bitch treated well in advance of her next season when the following remedies will be found useful:

1. *SEPIA 30c.* This remedy has the ability of regulating the function of the entire reproductive tract. It will have a tonic effect on the uterus in general and reduce the likelihood of chronic inflammatory processes giving trouble at parturition.

2. *HYDRASTIS 30c.* This is an excellent remedy for reducing catarrhal inflammation of the endometrium which leads to the discharge of catarrhal exudate.

3. *SILICEA 30c.* If there has been a history of previous inflammations which have resulted in the formation of scar tissue in the uterus, this remedy will help resolve such tissue. It will also be of benefit in controlling any chronic infections which may be present.

4. *HELONIAS 30c.* The bitch may show extreme sacral weakness with a tendency to prolapse of uterus. She may drag her hind quarters along the ground and it is a useful remedy in those cases which have developed as a result of a previous miscarriage.

5. *USTILAGO MAYDIS 30c.* A useful remedy in those cases where the uterus has hypertrophied as a result of succeeding inflammation and

has lost its tone. Haemorrhages are common from time to time, the blood appearing as long clots.

PYOMETRA, PYOMETRITIS
CYSTIC ENDOMETRIAL HYPERPLASIA

This condition may produce a large flaccid uterus or the organ may remain of normal size and show little change except bead-like swellings where cysts have developed in the endometrium. The great majority of cases which develop over a period show thinning of the uterine walls, the uterus itself containing fluid which is at first mucoid and later muco-purulent and evil-smelling. Pyometra is fairly common in the bitch and is more often seen in animals of middle and old age and in the maiden rather than in the animal which has had pups. There is a well recognised condition called pseudo or phantom pregnancy – a phase which may occur about six weeks to two months after oestrus and is often the forerunner of pyometritis. In this condition the endometrium becomes thickened and cysts of varying size appear on its surface. Hyperaemia and oedema occur due to glandular activity and while the uterine contents are at first sterile they quickly become contaminated by pyogenic bacteria which accounts for the toxaemia which invariably accompanies the condition. Two forms of pyometra are recognised: open and closed. The latter is the more dangerous in that escape of uterine contents is prevented and systemic involvement quickly follows. In the open type the uterine cervix remains patent and the condition is recognised by the escape of uterine contents, the discharge usually being purulent or haemorrhagic. Pyometra has become more prevalent since the practice of injecting bitching against misalliance has grown. This can lead to cystic hyperplasia if repeated too often.

CLINICAL SIGNS. The owner is at first concerned with the bitch showing increased thirst accompanying a pendulous abdomen and occasional vomiting. Discharge of muco-purulent and/or haemorrhagic exudate occurs in the open case and this is made manifest by the bitch licking the vulva frequently and staining of material where she lies or sleeps. Signs of toxaemia in the closed form include dehydration, dry lustreless coat and unpleasant body odour.

TREATMENT. In the absence or refusal of radical surgery, the following remedies will do much to improve the condition and alleviate or reduce the uterine contents. Many owners prefer this approach and if treatment is instituted in time the animal can be maintained in reasonably good health. The following remedies have all proved useful in different cases according to the character of the discharge and the nature of the animal:

1. HYDRASTIS 30c. This is a good general remedy when the open case shows the presence of catarrhal exudate in the early stages. It has a specific action on mucous membranes and reduces the amount of exudate which forms in the early inflammatory phase.

2. APIS MEL. 30c. Also useful in the early stages when inflammatory changes are attended by oedema.

3. SEPIA 30c. This remedy has an action on the entire genital tract helping to regulate its activity and controlling the hormonal imbalance which leads to the development of the condition.

4. CAULOPHYLLUM 30c. This remedy has a specific action on the uterus and should therefore be confined to open cases where it will be of great value in eliminating the purulent contents by stimulating uterine contractions. Discharges are frequently chocolate-coloured when this remedy is indicated.

5. CORPUS LUTEUM 30c. This potentised substance has proved useful in some cases when other remedies have been slow to produce results. It probably acts by regulating ovarian activity and reducing the likelihood of cysts developing in the endometrium.

6. OOPHERINUM 30c and PITUITARY 30c. Both these remedies will also help regulate ovarian activity and should be given alternately at monthly intervals between the animal's seasons.

Diseases and Problems incidental to the Brood Bitch

Failure to breed can have its origin in simple lack of oestrus or in conditions peculiar to the genital tract, e.g. metritis (including cervicitis) and vulvo-vaginitis (see previous chapter). Specific bacterial infections such as Brucellosis can also occur.

Animals which fail to exhibit a normal season may respond to the remedy *SEPIA 30c* which, as we have said earlier, has the power to regulate the entire genital function. Three doses at monthly intervals has been successful in many instances. A single dose of *PITUITRY 30c* will reinforce this.

BRUCELLOSIS

This infection has been reported in some kennels and is manifested by abortion at about seven weeks and also in a failure to breed afterwards. If this disease is proved to be present, all bitches should be given a course of *BRUCELLA NOSODE 30c* using the combined strains of abortus, melitensis and canis. One dose per month for three months should be administered to each bitch. Animals which have already been infected should receive a single dose together with a daily dose of *HEPAR SULPH. 30c* for two weeks. This will prove helpful in eliminating residual infection.

Non-specific abortions may also occur and those bitches which have a history of miscarriage should receive *SEPIA 30c*, one dose per month for three months, before subsequent mating. Once they have been mated and are thought to be in whelp, the following remedies will reduce the risk of miscarriage occurring: *1. VIBURNUM OP. 30c and 2. CAULOPHYLLUM 30c*. The former is more suitable in the early stages, e.g. about two weeks gestation, while the latter produces a more favourable result later in pregnancy. A single dose of Viburnum should suffice while two doses of Caulophyllum a week apart after the fourth week is sufficient.

Post-abortion discharges will yield to one or other of the following remedies.

1. SABINA 6c. Discharges are heavily blood-stained, the blood being bright red. There is a tendency to retention of placental material.

2. SECALE 30c. The blood is dark and fluid. The animal has a thin shrivelled appearance and is dehydrated. Extremities are cold.

3. SEPIA 30c. A useful remedy when there is a tendency to prolapse and the bitch is weak and listless. Discharges may or may not be present.

4. HYDRASTIS 30c. More useful in 'clean' abortions where the discharge is non-haemorrhagic and mainly muco-purulent.

5. LILIUM TIG. 30c. Discharges are thick, dark and clotted. There is severe straining accompanying diarrhoea and/or dysentery.

6. IPECACUANHA 30c. If bright red blood is passed in frequent gushes this remedy is probably more useful than any other.

7. PULSATILLA 30c. A suitable remedy for the affectionate bitch which shows changeability of symptoms, e.g. discharges alternating from haemorrhagic to muco-purulent.

CARE OF BITCH DURING PREGNANCY

Apart from normal diet and exercise, the administration of certain remedies will ensure the maintenance of pregnancy and reduce the likelihood of a difficult parturition. These include the following:

1. VIBURNUM OP. 30c. As we have already noted, this remedy given in the first two weeks of pregnancy helps to prevent miscarriage and is more suitable for animals which have shown a history of this.

2. CAULOPHYLLUM 30c. One dose of this remedy should be given every two weeks with a final dose during the last week. If there is difficulty at parturition with an *os uteri* which fails to dilate properly, it will bring about relaxation if given frequently for a few doses, e.g. one dose every half hour for four doses.

3. ARNICA 30c. Two doses of this remedy should be given in the final week of pregnancy. It will reduce the likelihood of damage to tissues at whelping and facilitate normal delivery. It should also be used post-partum when it will be instrumental in restoring tone to the birth canal.

4. SEPIA 30c. A single dose of this remedy after whelping will ensure that the uterus quickly returns to normal and will thus prevent straining and tendency to prolapse.

ECLAMPSIA. LACTATION OR PUERPERAL TETANY

This condition occurs occasionally and produces a tetany of muscles together with involvement of CNS. It is more common in bitches of small breeds, and is associated with large litters and a plentiful supply of milk.

ETIOLOGY. This is related to the calcium metabolism and has its origin in malfunction of the parathyroid gland. The exciting cause is a drop in the blood calcium level together with a correspondingly high Phosphorus level.

CLINICAL SIGNS. Symptoms generally appear about 10 to 14 days after parturition, occasionally later. The bitch soon becomes distressed, showing increased difficulty in respiration with anxiety and possibly whimpering. Signs of nervousness appear such as restlessness and excitement. Stiffness of movement occurs as a result of the upset Ca. metabolism. This leads to an inability to stand with rigidity of leg muscles apparent. True muscular tremors are seen, and these eventually lead to involvement of the CNS when convulsions set in. At this stage generalised constitutional signs appear such as discoloration of visible mucous membranes, high temperature and increased pulse of a wiry nature.

TREATMENT. The subcutaneous or intravenous injections of suitable Ca. salts generally bring about resolution but these measures should be supplemented by the use of the following remedies:

1. *BELLADONNA 200.* 2. *ACONITE 12x.* 3. *CALC. PHOS. 30c.* 4. *CURARE 30c.* 5. *STRAMONIUM 30c.* 6. *HYOSCAMUS 30c.*

PREVENTION OF PUERPERAL TETANY

There is less likelihood of the condition arising if the bitch is given a short course of *CALC. PHOS. 30c*, one per day after parturition is completed, together with a single dose of *PARATHYROID 30c*. This should help stabilise the Ca. metabolism and prevent undue loss in the milk. If there has been a history of previous attacks the administration of *CALC. PHOS. 30c* during pregnancy, one dose per week for the second month, will be an additional insurance.

DISEASES OF THE MAMMARY GLANDS

a) ACUTE MASTITIS. This condition is sometimes seen following parturition when one or more glands become swollen, hot and tender to the touch. The milk becomes curdled and yellow after a while, and in neglected cases discoloration of the mammary region occurs. The bitch is obviously in pain and discomfort and has an anxious expression.

TREATMENT. The following remedies have all proved useful:

1. ACONITUM 12x. Should be given in the early stages if possible. It will reduce anxiety and help calm the patient.

2. BELLADONNA 200c. Indicated when the glands are swollen, hot and tense. Constitutional symptoms such as dilated pupils and a full bounding pulse are present. Increased sensitivity or hyper-excitability may be seen.

3. APIS MEL. 30c. If the condition is seen at the stage of oedematous swelling soon after parturition, this remedy will help by reducing the tissue fluid and easing the pain.

4. PHYTOLACCA 30c. This is a valuable remedy as it has a selective action on the mammary gland. The inflammation may take the form of nodular patches of hard tissue while clots in the milk usually disappear under its influence.

5. BRYONIA 30c. Useful remedy when the gland is excessively hard while there may be an attendant constipation and respiratory upset such as pleurisy. General stiffness of limbs is present.

6. HEPAR SULPH. 200c. This remedy should be given when the bitch exhibits external aversion to touch indicating excessive tenderness and pain. Mammary secretion is probably thin and purulent.

7. *URTICA URENS 1x*. This remedy will help promote the flow of milk after acute symptoms have died down and the glands are returning to normal.

8. *S.S.C. 30c*. This is a compound remedy containing Sulphur, Silicea and Carbo Veg. It was first proved useful in the treatment of mastitis in cattle. The milk usually contains small pinhead size clots and the remedy is more useful in the less acute phase.

9. *PYROGEN 1M*. This remedy will be useful when constitutional involvement such as septicaemia arises. Indications for its use are a high temperature accompanying a weak thready pulse; a disagreeable odour is present with a cold body surface.

FOOTNOTE. B.B.U. 30c. This is a combination of Belladonna, Bryonia and Urtica Urens. It has proved useful in acute cases.

b) **MAMMARY TUMOURS.** These are frequently seen in the bitch which has not been spayed and commence as small nodular lumps varying in size from a pea to a walnut. At first benign, they have a tendency to become malignant as they develop.

Treatment is normally surgical but the following remedies may keep them in check in the early stages when they are beginning to develop:

1. *PHYTOLACCA 30c*. This remedy has an important action on the mammary tissue and will prove useful in reducing the size and hardness of the growth.

2. *CONIUM 30c*. A useful remedy when there are accompanying swellings of lymph glands and signs of muscular weakness. More suitable for the older animal.

3. *IODUM 30c*. Tumours are mainly superficial together with shrinking of mammary tissue when Iodum is indicated. The subject most suited to this remedy may be thin with a dry shrivelled-looking coat and possessing a voracious appetite. Superficial lymph glands are small and hard.

4. *BROMIUM 30c*. The left side of the mammary area is more affected when this remedy is indicated. Pressure over the glands is resented. There are accompanying respiratory symptoms such as coughing and nasal discharge.

5. *PLUMBUM IOD. 30c.* May be needed when there are attendant symptoms of paresis or incipient paralysis. The glands are usually stone hard and constipation is a constant feature.

6. *SCROPHULARIA NODOSA 30c.* This remedy has a beneficial effect on the glandular system generally, and has given good results in helping to disperse small nodular growths.

7. *CARCINOSIN 200c.* This is the carcinoma nosode and should be given as an additional remedy. A single dose should suffice when combined with the appropriate remedy.

Diseases of the
Male Reproductive System

Many conditions affecting this system are surgical in nature but homoeopathy can help in some of the more functional complaints such as inflammatory affections of penis, testes and prostate gland. These can be outlined as follows:

1. BALANITIS

This is the term used to denote inflammation of the glans penis and is relatively common. It is characterised by the presence of a purulent exudate together with a swelling of the glans. There may be systemic symptoms such as elevated temperature and increased pulse rate in severe cases. The main remedies to be considered are as follows:

1. ACONITUM 12c. Should be given first in any acute manifestation especially if systemic symptoms arise.

2. BELLADONNA 30c. When symptoms of dilated pupils, fast throbbing pulse and a hot skin are present, this remedy will help systemic cases of this nature.

3. MERC. SOL. 6c. This is the main remedy to consider in uncomplicated cases especially if the exudate is of a greenish colour as it very often is.

4. MERC. CORR. 30c. Useful for the more serious or intractable case where the previous remedy has given only moderate results.

5. THUJA 6c. This remedy may be needed after a course of *MERC.* as it has a deep action and will act constitutionally.

6. ACID. NIT. 30c. If the glans is affected by vesicles or ulcers, this remedy may be particularly helpful, and will also help if inflammatory changes have affected the sheath.

7. In all cases the parts should be bathed regularly with a 1/10 solution of *CALENDULA.*

2. ORCHITIS

This term denotes inflammation of the testicles and is less common than the preceding complaint. One or both testicles may be affected. In the acute form the gland becomes swollen, tender and hot and abscess formation may supervene. Chronic orchitis results in a hardening of the gland tissue leading to fibrotic changes. Treatment consists of giving simple food and allowing plenty of rest, together with consideration of one or other of the following remedies:

1. PULSATILLA 6c. Sometimes only one testicle is involved when this remedy is indicated. The inflammation extends upwards towards the inguinal canal. There may be dropsical signs present, while systemic symptoms include vomiting. Signs of hypersexuality may be seen.

2. RHODODODENDRON 6c. Indicated when the testicles are extremely painful on touch, and they appear retracted. Itching is usually present, manifested by the animal gnawing at the parts.

3. HEPAR SULPH. 30c. Also indicated when the testicles are extremely sensitive to touch, but in this case abscess formation is usually beginning. Higher potencies may abort the suppurative process.

4. BRYONIA 6c. A useful remedy when the gland substance is hard and pressure eases the condition. The animal may be seen lying on the abdomen in an endeavour to bring pressure to bear on the area.

5. IODUM 30c. A useful remedy in the chronic form where the gland structure appears shrivelled and the organs themselves reduced in size.

6. SILICEA 30c. Should be considered when fibrous changes have appeared in the gland structure, evidenced by firmness and coldness of the gland.

7. BRUCELLA CANIS 30c. If brucellosis infection has been proved as a contributory factor, the intercurrent use of this nosode will help.

3. ENLARGED PROSTATE GLAND

This represents a hypertrophic enlargement dependent on hormonal changes and is fairly common in the older dog which still has functioning testicles. The enlarged gland may contain cysts which give it a nodular feel. These also give the urine a discoloured appearance due to the presence of cystic fluid and cause the albumen content to increase. Main remedies to consider if cystic hypertrophy is present include:

1. *APIS MEL. 30c* which will help reduce cystic fluid.

2. *FERRUM PIC. 6c.* This is a good general remedy to be considered in all cases of prostatic enlargement.

3. *SOLIDAGO 30c.* This is also an excellent remedy especially when unsuccessful attempts at micturition are present indicating hypertrophy.

Acute inflammation of the gland can arise independently of any enlargement and is usually due to infection of one kind or another, giving rise to constitutional symptoms such as elevated temperature and increased pulse rate. The animal usually adopts a posture with back arched, which position appears to afford relief. Rectal examination is resented. Treatment of such acute manifestation includes the following remedies:

1. *ACONITUM 30c.* To be considered in all early stages when its use will relieve anxiety and help calm the animal.

2. *BELLADONNA 30c.* If the usual symptoms of dilated pupils, throbbing pulse and body heat are present, this remedy will be indicated.

3. *HEPAR SULPH. 200c.* In this strength the remedy will help allay the tendency to abscess formation.

4. *CHIMAPHILLA UMBELLATA. 6c.* Swelling in the perineal area is present along with slimy ropy mucus in the urine. Passage of urine is extremely difficult.

The question of **ANAL ADENOMATA** in the elderly male animal may be considered here. These are tumours which develop in the peri-anal region and commence as hard pea-like swellings which eventually coalesce and become malignant in due course. They are extremely difficult to treat medically but the remedies *ACID. NIT. 30c*, *CALC. FLUOR. 30c* and *STILBOESTROL 30c.* have proved useful, in many cases helping to arrest the growth of the adenoma.

4. IMPOTENCY

Inability or unwillingness to mate is not often met with but if it is desired to treat such a condition success may attend the use of remedies such as *LYCOPODIUM 1M, AGNUS CASTUS 6c, DAMIANA 6c* or *STAPHISAGRIA 6c*. Strictly speaking, stud dogs developing this tendency should not be bred from as there is a possibility that the condition could develop in their offspring after they have been treated successfully.

Allergic Diseases

1. ANAPHYLAXIS

This is a hypersensitive state which can be brought on by contact with some specific antigen or by the dog receiving antibodies from another animal, e.g. by serum injection. Also certain tissues may contain substances which are conducive to an anaphylactic attack.

CLINICAL SIGNS. It may be seen as a local or widespread inflammatory process ranging from arteriole contraction with circulatory weakness to the onset of severe pathological states. Actual anaphylactic shock in the dog is frequently attended by vomiting, diarrhoea and severe prostration, and arises very quickly as a rule, after exposure to the antigen concerned, usually hyper-immune serum. Other signs include difficult respiration, loss of balance and paleness of visible mucous membranes.

TREATMENT. If it is possible to supply aid in time, the following remedies may help:

1. ACONITUM 6c. This remedy should be given immediately as it will help combat shock, especially in cases which show suddenness of onset.

2. CAMPHORA 30c. A very useful remedy for collapsed states showing diarrhoea and extreme coldness of body surfaces. Stools are watery and dark and attacks of diarrhoea arise suddenly.

3. CARBO VEG. 200c. When signs of air hunger or dyspnoea appear this remedy will benefit. It has a sound reputation for giving strength and warmth to apparently moribund cases.

4. VERATRUM ALB. 30c. This remedy is also useful in cases of collapse with prostration and diarrhoea, but unlike the *CAMPHOR* picture, symptoms are less severe. Stools tend to be greenish.

2. ALLERGIC CONTACT DERMATITIS

This is the term used for those cases of hypersensitivity — often delayed — when the dog shows a reaction to an agent which contacts the skin, such agent being of a non-irritating nature. Exposure to the particular agent is usually prolonged and the animal must have a predisposition to the condition.

CLINICAL SIGNS. Lesions usually are confined to the hairless parts such as the inner legs, scrotum or inguinal area and the interdigital spaces. Erythematous swellings at first develop which later become papular. Severe cases will include most parts of the body as well.

TREATMENT. The following remedies should prove useful:

1. ANTIMONIUM CRUD. 6c. Useful for the papular stage of the lesion and will help prevent development to vesicles.

2. RHUS TOX. 6c. For the early erythematous stage before papules develop. Itching may be severe.

3. CORTISONE 30c. This substance in potentised form has proved very useful in controlling the inflammatory process without producing any side-effects.

4. THALLIUM ACETAS 30c. A most useful remedy encouraging hair growth and for stimulating the skin functions in general.

5. SPECIFIC NOSODE MADE FROM THE AGENT RESPONSIBLE. This should be used in the 30c. potency and may be combined with other indicated remedies.

3. CAR SICKNESS

Under this heading we can consider any motion which brings about symptoms of discomfort to the animal on experiencing travel, and includes air and sea-sickness as well as the much commoner car sickness.

CLINICAL SIGNS. Signs of distress soon become apparent after transportation begins, and include panting, salivation and vomiting. Sometimes bowel evacuation takes place also. Signs of inappetance and distress may continue for some little time after the journey has finished, and are probably accompanied by nausea as in the human subject.

TREATMENT. Animals should not be subjected to car or air journeys immediately after a meal. It is a good plan to keep the animal on the floor of the vehicle where it cannot see out of the window, as visual disturbances are thought to play a part in the onset of symptoms. The main remedy to be considered is *COCCULUS 6c* or *30c*. If a dose of this remedy is given about 15 minutes before commencement of the journey it will greatly reduce the likelihood of vomiting. *TABACUM 30c* is another useful remedy and more suitable perhaps for air or sea-sickness.

Diseases of the Eye

These fall into different categories and include affections of the eyelids, conjunctiva, cornea and retina particularly.

1. THE EYELIDS

a) BLEPHARITIS. This is the term used to describe simple inflammation of the eyelids and can take various forms, e.g. ulcerative, seborrhoeal and pyogenic. In simple acute blepharitis the lids become swollen and oedematous giving the eye a puffy look. The ulcerative form is accompanied by vesicles on the skin of the eyelids. These rupture and give rise to ulcers, which shed a greyish discharge. In the seborrhoeal form the skin becomes red and thickened and there are usually skin lesions elsewhere on the body. There may be dandruff-like flakes present on the skin. Pyogenic blepharitis is associated with Staphylococcal infection giving rise to small abscesses here and there and dependent on systemic infection, e.g. from Distemper or any condition leading to a conjunctivitis.

TREATMENT. The simple form showing oedema and puffiness should respond to *APIS MEL. 30c* followed by *RHUS TOX. 6c* and *1M.* If it is thought to be due to some extraneous factor, e.g. allergy, the remedy *URTICA URENS 6x* should help.

Ulcerative blepharitis may need treatment with *RANUNCULUS BULBOSUS 6c, ANTIMONIUM CRUD. 6c, ACID. NIT. 30c, KALI BICH. 6c* and the nosode *VARIOLINUM 30c*, depending on overall symptoms displayed. Reference should be made to a standard Materia Medica to determine which, although *ACID. NIT.* usually gives good results being a remedy which exerts a beneficial action on conditions affecting areas where skin and mucous membranes meet. The pyogenic form should be controlled by the use of the nosode *STAPHYLOCOCCUS 30c* along with selected remedies such as *MERC. CORR. 6c, PULSATILLA 6c* and *HEPAR SULPH. 30c*

137

although other less likely remedies may also be needed. In all cases the eyelids should be bathed with a dilute solution of *CALENDULA*.

b) ENTROPION and ECTROPION. The turning in or out of the eyelids is sometimes met with in certain breeds, e.g. Chow and Boxer, and, while surgical interference is usually required for correction, the remedy *BORAX 6c or 30c* has given good results in mild cases and should always be given a try before surgery is attempted. Treatment should be given over a period of three months (see Preface for general rules on frequency etc.).

c) HORDEOLUM. This is the technical name given to the condition known as Stye, which is a roundish swelling usually found at the inner edge of the eyelid. It is attended by pain and discomfort with lachrymation.

TREATMENT. One of the best remedies for this condition is *STAPHISAGRIA 6c*, although remedies such as *CALC. FLUOR. 30c* and *SILICEA 30c* may be needed for more stubborn or long-standing cases. If attended by undue pain and sensitivity, *HEPAR SULPH. 30c* is indicated.

d) CHALAZION. This is the term used to denote the presence of a chronic painless nodule or swelling situated along the margin of the eyelid. The main remedies to be considered in the absence of surgical removal are *CALC. FLUOR. 30c*, *SILICEA 30c* and *THUJA 30c*.

e) DACRYOCYSTITIS. Inflammation of the lachrymal ducts may be associated with a chronic conjunctivitis resulting from bacterial infection. The main clinical sign consists of a swelling at the inner canthus of the eye. Pressure over the area may reveal the presence of pus. Treatment consists of giving one or other of the following remedies depending on severity and stage of the condition, e.g. *HEPAR SULPH. 30c* for those cases exhibiting extreme tenderness, *SILICEA 30c* for the more long-standing case, *ARGENT. NIT. 6c* if there is an associated conjunctivitis, *PULSATILLA 6c* where there is an abundance of creamy pus, *LEDUM 6c* and *SYMPHYTUM 200c* if there is a history of injury to the eye. The eye should be bathed with a dilute (1/10) solution of *HYPERCAL* (Hypericum and Calendula).

2. THE CONJUNCTIVA

CONJUNCTIVITIS. This is the name given to inflammation of the inner surface of the eyelids and usually refers to the palpebral area. It is of fairly common occurrence, and may be unilateral or bilateral. The latter is usually seen if the condition is allergic in origin. The main clinical signs are increased vascularity giving a deep red appearance. Oedema is usually present and a clear mucous discharge may appear, becoming purulent if secondary bacterial infection takes place. Treatment consists of bathing the eye with a 1/10 solution of *CALENDULA/HYPERICUM* to clear away any discharge. This will also soothe the conjunctival surfaces. This should be followed again with a 1/10 solution of *EUPHRASIA* which has a tonic effect on all eye structures. Internally there is a variety of useful remedies to consider, chief among which are *ARGENT. NIT. 6c*, *PULSATILLA 30c*, *LEDUM 6c*, *SYMPHYTUM 200c*, *RHUS TOX. 6c*, *ARNICA 30c*, *HEPAR SULPH. 30c*, and *MERC. SOL. 6c*.

FOOTNOTE. Acute catarrhal conjunctivitis may accompany the early stages of Canine Distemper or Canine Hepatitis infection and treatment may have to be changed to take this into account. (See chapter on Virus Diseases.)

3. THE CORNEA

The main conditions to consider are simple erosion, inflammation (Keratitis) and ulceration. In simple erosion the cornea loses its sheen and appears dull. Lachrymation is present along with a degree of conjunctivitis. Treatment should be directed towards easing the discomfort by bathing with *HYPERCAL* or *EUPHRASIA*, diluting the mother tincture 1/10. Internally the remedies *SYMPHYTUM 200c* and *LEDUM 6c* should help. Corneal ulceration is not uncommon and is sometimes referred to as Ulcerative Keratitis. Frequently these ulcers are the result of an external injury but sometimes they arise independently of any obvious injury. The ulcers are usually centrally placed and can become secondarily infected with pyogenic bacteria.

Clinical signs are obvious and are accompanied by an aversion to light. The main remedies to consider in treatment are *ACID. NIT. 30c* or *200c*, *LEDUM 6c*, *KALI BICH. 6c*, *MERC. CORR. 30c* and *SYMPHYTUM 200c*, all of which have been used with success according to selective symptoms. Externally the ulcers should be bathed with *HYPERCAL* 1/10 followed by *EUPHRASIA Ø* 1/10.

Opacities of the cornea show as a cloudy film across the eye and may respond well to the remedies *CANNABIS SAT. 6c*, *CALC. FLUOR. 30c* and *SILICEA 30c*. The early inflammatory stage of Keratitis may be treated with *ARGENT. NIT. 6c*, *LEDUM 6c* and *PHOS. 30c*. These remedies should be helpful in preventing the condition developing into a more chronic form leading to ulceration and opacity.

4. THE UVEA

The vascular layer of the eye which includes the iris, ciliary body and the choroid is referred to as the Uvea. Inflammation of any of these structures is referred to as Uveitis and chief among these is that affecting the iris and ciliary body (Iridocyclitis), which can arise as a sequel to infection from wounds or from extension of a corneal ulcer. The condition may be acute or chronic, the former showing as increased vascularity with exudation of the iris and ciliary body. The pupils are constricted and there is aversion to light. Exudation of aqueous material which includes white cells gives a clouded appearance to the eye. More chronic forms exhibit adhesions between the iris and the lens while disturbance of local circulation can lead on to glaucoma. Treatment should be attempted by considering one or other of the following remedies: *ACONITUM 30c* in the early stages if possible, *LEDUM 6c*, *SYMPHYTUM 200c* and *PHOSPHORUS 30c*.

5. THE LENS

The chief condition affecting the lens is cataract, which is frequently seen as dogs become old and is a condition which may be congenital or acquired. Cataracts may assume different shapes, and can prove refractory to medical treatment. Chief among remedies which have proved successful in early stages are *CONIUM MAC.*, *SILICEA*,

CALC. FLUOR., *NAT. MUR.* and *PHOSPHORUS*. Differing potencies of these may be needed. Externally a useful application is *CINERARIA* Ø diluted 1/10, a few drops being applied daily for a week or two in conjunction with an internal remedy. The specific form of cataract associated with Diabetes may be responsive to treatment for that disease.

6. THE RETINA

The main conditions which need concern us are Progressive Retinal atrophy and Glaucoma, both of which are extremely difficult to treat.

Retinal atrophy may be termed generalised or central and some breeds are susceptible to one kind and some to the other. Clinical signs of the generalised form include reduced night vision and afterwards a reduction in day vision. The pupils become dilated as the disease progresses and cataracts may develop. The central form is seen more in the younger age group, and early signs in this case show the animal apparently unable to see objects close at hand, although evidently able to see those at a distance. The main remedy to consider if treatment is attempted is *PHOSPHORUS*. Although it is impossible to correct any degeneration which has already taken place, some animals have shown a response to this remedy in that further degeneration has been halted. Other remedies which could be applicable include *HAMAMELIS* and *CROTALUS HORR.* but the author has no experience of their use in this connection.

Glaucoma represents a condition where damage to the retina and optic nerve is brought about by an increase in intraocular pressure due to a build up of the vitreous humour. It is usually secondary to some other disease or affection of the eye such as uveitis. Acute and chronic congestive forms have been noted, the former showing as reddening of the conjunctiva with a watery discharge with the eye partly shut. Palpation of the eyeball is resented. The cornea becomes severely clouded. The chronic state follows on from the acute in the absence of treatment and the whole eye is greatly enlarged, the blood-vessels being markedly engorged. The cornea may become thickened and possibly ulcerated. Treatment of glaucoma can frequently be unrewarding but the following remedies are worthy of consideration:

ACONITUM in the early stages, followed by *BELLADONNA*. *APIS MEL*. will have a beneficial effect by helping to reduce the oedema present, while remedies such as *SPIGELIA* and *COLOCYNTHIS* will help to relieve the pain which often accompanies the acute stage. *PHOSPHORUS* is another remedy which may give good results in the more chronic stage.

Diseases of the Ear

Chief among conditions affecting the ears which claim our attention are the various types of inflammation known as Otitis Externa, Media, and Interna. In the dog the first of these is by far the most important, although extension to the middle and inner ear structures can occur from affections of the external areas or auditory canal. The various conditions are commonly referred to as Ear Canker.

1. OTITIS EXTERNA (see also chapter on Skin)

This extremely common condition may range from a simple reddening and mild inflammation of the outer canal to thickening of the epithelial tissue inside the ear flap. It is referred to as acute or chronic. The acute form may show simply undue warmth or be attended by ulceration and suppuration or again simply by an increase in wax content. The chronic condition leads to thickening of the outer ear flap which also may show ulceration.

ETIOLOGY. The various factors implicated in the development of Otitis Externa include narrowness of the ear canal, the presence of undue quantities of hair (as in the Poodle) and long drooping ears (as in the Spaniel). The presence of fluid in the canal can also contribute to it. Frequently the cause is systemic and in this case is often associated with the development of ezcematous lesions elsewhere.

CLINICAL SIGNS. The early stages produce an increase in wax which becomes soft and semi-fluid and arises as a direct result of inflammatory changes. As the condition develops or if treatment is neglected, secondary infection gains entrance to the auditory canal and gives rise to suppuration with the production of a purulent exudate.

Chronic Otitis Externa, besides giving rise to proliferative changes which can be attended by ulceration, frequently also gives rise to a dermatitis of the adjacent tissues including the outer ear flap. The first obvious sign is shaking of the head or pawing at the affected ear. The

143

head is held on the side (towards the affected ear) giving the head a tilted appearance. Examination reveals an increase in wax with redness and possibly ulceration of the lining of the canal. More severe forms show purulent exudate of an evil-smelling nature together with thickening of the epithelium. Scratching of the ear results in many cases in a dermatitis of the adjoining ear flap.

TREATMENT. There are many excellent remedies available for the various stages which may arise:

1. *ACONITUM 30c.* Should be given in the very early stages when the ear shows an initial redness and warmth. It will help allay distress.

2. *BELLADONNA 30c.* An excellent remedy also in the early stage when the ear is hot, throbbing and swollen.

3. *ARSEN. ALB. 6c.* This is a useful remedy when there is a thin serous discharge from the ear. The animal shows a desire for warmth and is usually restless. Symptoms tend to be exacerbated towards midnight.

4. *RHUS TOX. 6c.* The ear flap is hot and shows slight vesicular or papular involvement. The left ear is more affected than the right.

5. *TELLURIUM 30c.* This is an excellent general remedy for ear conditions. The ear flap may show thickening and eczematous lesions which can extend to the outer covering.

6. *HEPAR SULPH. 30c.* Pain is evident from the animal showing resentment at being touched. The inflammation is usually deep-seated and excess semi-liquid wax is present.

7. *MERC. SOL. 30c.* A useful remedy when early changes have given way to the suppurative stage, with the production of a greenish discharge. A heavy musty smell is present.

8. *MERC. CORR. 30c.* Indicated in the more severe suppurative form when blood may be present in the purulent exudate. There are frequently systemic eczematous lesions present with possibly mucous diarrhoea at night.

9. *PSORINUM 30c.* This nosode may be needed in the dirty-coated, chilly animal which exhibits excessive scratching producing a musty smell. The coat is usually harsh and dry.

FOOTNOTE. The ear should be bathed with a dilute solution (1/10) of Hypercal (Hypericum and Calendula tincture) or Hydrogen Peroxide.

Endocrine Diseases

Many of the diseases affecting the endocrine glands are outwith the scope of homoeopathic or other treatment, consisting in many cases of tumours which affect the function of the glands and lead to over or under-activity. Tumours of the pituitary gland are not uncommon and can lead to malfunction of other glands. The glands which concern us as regards treatment are the pancreas, the posterior pituitary and the adrenals giving rise to Diabetes mellitus, Diabetes insipidus and Cushing's syndrome. Disturbances of thyroid function are also not uncommon but conventional replacement therapy in hypothyroidism is entirely adequate, while hyper-thyroidism (Graves' Disease) is infrequently observed.

1. THE PANCREAS

This gland has a double function in that it produces a hormone insulin which controls sugar metabolism (the endocrine function) and also digestive enzymes (the exocrine function). Conditions affecting the latter function — pancreatitis, have already been referred to under the heading Digestive Diseases and we shall here concentrate on the endocrine function, in essence that of hypofunction, viz Diabetes mellitus.

DIABETES MELLITUS. This disease can take a long time to manifest itself clinically and appears to be increasing among the canine population especially among bitches over five years of age.

ETIOLOGY. The primary cause is a decrease in the amount of the hormone insulin secreted and this in turn depends on many other factors including the role played by the pituitary gland.

CLINICAL SIGNS. Symptoms may develop insidiously and are frequently advanced by the time professional help is sought. Loss of weight and excessive drinking are the usual signs which first attract attention. The appetite is usually well-maintained while cataract and skin lesions are more or less constant complications in severe cases. The liver is also affected leading to acidosis as a result of incomplete combustion of fats.

TREATMENT. It must be clearly understood that the selection of remedies outlined is not intended to replace insulin therapy, but merely to supplement this. However, mild cases may respond to careful diet and remedies as needed. Among the more commonly employed remedies are the following:

1. SYZYGIUM 3x. Indicated when there is increased passage of urine which has a high sugar content. Thirst is usually pronounced.

2. SILICEA 30c. This remedy may help cases which have developed cataract.

3. CALC. FLUOR. 30c. A good tissue remedy which also will have a beneficial effect in opacities of the eye structures.

4. URANIUM NIT. 30c. Indicated when there is profuse nocturnal urination, the urine being pale and milky-looking. Sugar in the urine is usually preceded by albuminuria.

5. IRIS VERS. 30c. When this remedy is indicated there are soft yellowish stools accompanying a urine of a high specific gravity. It is a good pancreatic remedy in general.

6. IODUM 30c. The urine may be deep yellowish-green and have a milky appearance. Bowel motions are loose and pale, sometimes frothy and yellow with a mushy consistency.

7. PANCREATIN 30c. The intercurrent use of the pancreas nosode will aid the action of selected remedies.

2. THE POSTERIOR PITUITARY GLAND

DIABETES INSIPIDUS. This affection is manifested by the animal producing large amounts of clear dilute urine; at the same time large quantities of water are drunk. It is more common in the older animal.

ETIOLOGY. Many cases are due to lesions affecting the posterior lobe of the pituitary gland and associated structures but others arise without any cause having been established.

CLINICAL SIGNS. The owner's attention is drawn to the large amounts of water consumed and the correspondingly large output of clear dilute urine of a very low specific gravity. The onset may be gradual or signs may appear suddenly. Output of urine may increase during the hours of darkness. There is an overall dry appearance of the coat, while visible mucous membranes together with the mouth and tongue appear dry.

TREATMENT. It is rare for a permanent cure to be effected but the polyuria and excessive drinking can be controlled to a large extent by the use of appropriate remedies. Chief among these are the following:

1. URANIUM NIT. 30c. This remedy has a beneficial action on pancreas function generally. The urine varies between high and low specific gravity depending on food partaken.

2. ACETIC ACID 30c. When this remedy is indicated the abdomen is distended and the urine contains phosphates. There is an accompanying diarrhoea.

3. ALFALFA 6x. A bloated abdomen with urine containing increased urea and phosphates may indicate the need for this remedy. Stools are loose and yellow.

4. CANNABIS IND. 30c. The animal may have difficulty in passing urine which is slow to come. The urine itself is again pale. Yellowish diarrhoea is present.

5. EUPATORIUM PURPUREUM 30c. Passage of urine is increased at night. The urine contains deposits of lithates.

6. APOCYNUM CANN. 30c. The urine is copious and passed almost involuntarily. There are no deposits present.

7. ACID. PHOS. 30c. On standing the urine becomes thick and cloudy. There may be tenderness over the lumbar region and uneasiness before passage of urine.

8. CORTICOTROPHIN (A.C.T.H.) 30c. The potentised steroid will

147

materially aid the action of other remedies and can be given as an intercurrent remedy.

3. THE ADRENAL GLANDS

The only condition which need concern us here is that brought about by an increase in the function of the adrenal cortex — a syndrome which goes by the name of Cushing's Disease.

ETIOLOGY OF CUSHING'S DISEASE. This condition is brought on by excessive production of the steroid hormones produced by the outer layer (cortex) of the adrenal gland. It is seen more in dogs over seven years old and can affect all breeds.

CLINICAL SIGNS. Enlargement of the abdominal cavity is an early sign together with a dry appearance of the coat which progresses to weakness of the hair follicles leading to loss of hair. This is seen on both flanks giving a symmetrical appearance to the lesions and extends to other areas including the front of the legs, behind the ears and in the flexions of the joints. The tail is also affected. As the condition worsens the abdomen increases in size. Skin lesions are also common, pimply rashes occurring on rough scaly surfaces. Blood examination reveals a decrease in the number of white cells of the lymphocyte and eosinophil types.

TREATMENT. The main remedies to be considered are as follows:

1. CORTICOTROPHIN (A.C.T.H.) 30c. This hormone has given good results in treatment, helping to reduce the excess of fluid which is sometimes present in the tissues and generally improving the adrenal function.

2. CORTISONE 30c. This hormone in potency will also assist in counteracting the effects of over-production of the crude hormone.

3. THALLIUM ACETAS 30c. This remedy has a trophic action on the skin and hair follicles and should help restore a healthy coat.

FOOTNOTE. It should be noted that the indiscrimate use or over-administration of Cortisone and other steroid hormones can produce a clinical picture indistinguishable from the actual disease. This is frequently seen after prolonged steroid treatment in skin disease. This represents a serious hazard to homoeopathic prescribing as remedies will not act properly in the presence of these drugs if present in excess. The use of the potentised hormone along with remedies such as NUX VOMICA and THUJA will help overcome this.

Bacterial Diseases

1. TETANUS

Although dogs are rather resistant to infection the disease will follow the usual pattern once the toxin reaches the central nervous system.

ETIOLOGY. The causative organism is a bacterium called Clostridium tetani, a sporulating bacillus which is anaerobic, i.e. it flourishes in the absence of free oxygen.

CLINICAL SIGNS. Any penetrating wound can give rise to tetanus, especially when the point of entry quickly becomes sealed over denying the entry of air and if the penetrating object is rusty or dirty. There is an incubation period up to eight days following wound infection. Muscular spasms of varying degree and frequency occur before the toxin has entered the central nervous system. These spasms lead to various abnormalities and deformities such as prolapse of the third eyelid, retraction of lips and upper eyelids and stretching of the body. The entry of the toxin into the nervous system is first ushered in by an increased sensitivity to external stimuli. The further away from the central nervous system of the original wound the longer it will be before symptoms occur.

TREATMENT. All of the following remedies may be needed at different stages:

1. LEDUM 6c. This is a main remedy following the infliction of any deep punctured wound. It is especially helpful if the area surrounding the wound becomes cold and discoloured.

2. HYPERICUM 1M. This remedy has a special affinity for the nervous system and its early administration should help to limit the spread of toxin to the peripheral nerves and its subsequent passage to the spinal cord. It may be alternated with the previous remedy in the early stages.

3. STRYCHNINUM 30c. When excessive muscle contractions occur this remedy will be needed. The back is frequently bent or arched and the patient extends the legs as far as possible.

4. CURARE 30c. Indicated when there is generalised muscle stiffness, especially of the neck and shoulders. The head is drawn back.

5. GELSEMIUM 30c. Milder cases showing muscular weakness and disinclination to move may respond to this remedy. The animal may have a sleepy look.

6. TETANUS NOSODE 30c. Should be given as an intercurrent remedy along with any of the above.

2. LEPTOSPIROSIS. WEIL'S DISEASE.

This disease may take various forms ranging from acute to chronic and is frequently sudden in onset.

ETIOLOGY. The causal organism is a spirochaete, the main species responsible being L. icterohaemorrhagica and L. canicola.

EPIZOOTIOLOGY. These organisms are widespread in nature and transmission to dogs takes place through the medium of contaminated rat urine. Penetration can also take place through skin abrasions. Excretion in the urine can last for many months after recovery.

CLINICAL SIGNS. In the acute form onset can be very sudden and the animal is first seen vomiting and passing loose motions. Loss of appetite and a dehydrated appearance set in. The coat becomes harsh and dry and walking is attended with difficulty, signs of stiffness being apparent over the sacral area. Pain is evident on abdominal palpation. The visible mucous membranes become congested but jaundice is an inconstant sign. Ulceration of the mucous membranes is a common feature. Gastrointestinal involvement takes the form of bile-stained vomiting together with dark-brown or blood-stained stools which may also contain whole blood. The presence of bile pigment may give the stool a greenish tinge. The respiratory system does not escape and coryza with coughing is a frequent symptom. The urine becomes dark and bile-stained.

TREATMENT. It is important that treatment be started as soon as possible. The following remedies appear indicated:

1.   ACONITUM 12x. Considering the sudden onset, this remedy is of first importance. It will allay shock and limit the progress of the disease.

2.   ARSEN. ALB. 30c. Should help control the gastro-intestinal symptoms and be of value in helping to overcome the dehydration which sets in.

3.   MERC. CORR. 30c. A very important remedy once ulcerations of buccal mucous membranes develop. Also indicated to control the mucous and blood-stained diarrhoea.

4.   BAPTISIA 30c. A remedy which may be needed to combat prostration and muscular soreness. Putrid excretions and exhalations particularly indicate its use. In the classical case this remedy may do better work than any other.

5.   CROTALUS HORR. 30c. If icteric or jaundice symptoms appear, Crotalus should be considered because of its action on liver function in septicaemic illnesses. It will also help control haemorrhagic tendencies.

6.   PHOSPHORUS 30c. Will help the coughing associated with respiratory involvement, and should have a beneficial effect on the liver leading to a reduction in vomiting.

7.   BERBERIS VULG. 30c. Another useful liver remedy which should have a beneficial effect on the bile metabolism. Under its action bile pigments should disappear from the urine and it will also help the stiffness which appears over the sacral area.

8.   LYCOPODIUM 1M. The chronic case exhibiting wasting and inappetance will be helped by this remedy. It has a long term beneficial action on liver function.

9.   LEPTOSPIROSIS NOSODE 30c. Should be given as an intercurrent agent along with any of the above remedies. Its use in the convalescent stages should prevent a build-up of leptospirae in the kidneys where their presence leads to the development of interstitial nephritis and excretion in the urine.

PREVENTION. *LEPTOSPIROSIS NOSODE* can be given either separately or in combination with *CANINE HEPATITIS* and *DISTEMPER NOSODES* over the same period of time.

3. EHRLICHIA CANIS INFECTION

This rickettsial disease affects both dogs and foxes.

ETIOLOGY. The disease is caused by a rickettsial organism by the name of E. canis.

EPIZOOTOLOGY. This organism is widespread in distribution and is transmitted by a vector tick, all developing stages of which harbour the rickettsia. This appears to be the only known mode of transmission.

CLINICAL SIGNS. There may be an incubation period of three weeks which ushers in a primary fever which may last a few days. Conjunctivitis can arise giving a muco-purulent discharge. The central nervous system is usually attacked with symptoms varying from mild ataxia to paraplegia and convulsions. There may also be diarrhoea and inappetance but these are not serious considerations in this disease.

TREATMENT.

1. ACONITUM 12x. As in other infectious conditions showing early fever, this remedy is always indicated.

2. PULSATILLA 6c. Should help control the ocular discharges especially if these show a tendency to change rapidly from serous to muco-purulent.

3. CONIUM 30c. The chief remedy for the ataxia which is the most prominent neurotoxic sign. Ascending potencies may be needed according to the degree of involvement from inco-ordination through to paraplegia.

4. BELLADONNA 1M. If convulsions set in, this is the main remedy to be considered.

Virus Diseases

1. DISTEMPER

This disease is of widespread occurrence and while the primary cause is a virus it is complicated by the appearance of symptoms and lesions due to secondary bacterial invasion.

EPIZOOTIOLOGY. The secretions and excretions exhibited by dogs in the early acute stage of this disease contain a virus which contaminates surrounding areas and is air-borne, causing transference to other susceptible animals. Young animals in the puppy stage are more at risk than the older dog, while foxes, ferrets and weasels can transmit the disease.

CLINICAL SIGNS. In the very young pup the only signs of disease may be diarrhoea, possibly blood-stained, and a disinclination to feed. These signs are the result of a haemorrhagic enteritis. Older puppies and dogs above four months of age exhibit a primary fever with a rise in temperature of 3° to 4°. In the classical form the nose is dry and hot and the eyes have an anxious expression. This is followed by a discharge from eyes and nose, at first watery and clear but later containing mucus and sometimes purulent material. Respiratory involvement starts with a soft moist cough and this particular type of cough has become almost pathognomonic of the disease. A harsh dry skin sometimes showing a papular or vesicular rash on the abdomen and inner flanks is usually a constant sign. Diarrhoea, usually blood-stained and foul smelling, is invariably present. If the disease is allowed to run its course or if early treatment has been ineffective, pneumonia develops and may take a severe form with rust-coloured sputum and nasal discharge. The majority of animals which linger on eventually show involvement of the nervous system in one form or another, ranging from muscular twitchings and chorea affecting cranial or peripheral nerves in milder cases to convulsions which become progressively more severe the longer the animal lives. The spinal cord may be affected more deeply, resulting in paralysis of varying degree. In very severe cases complete paraplegia may result. Involvement of the nervous system is usually accompanied by a thickening or induration of the foot pads. The commonest sequelae of unsuccessfully-treated cases are muscular twitchings (chorea) and varying degrees of paralysis. This is one of the most distressing aspects of the disease as the animal is invariably bright and usually maintains a good appetite.

TREATMENT. Homoeopathic medicine has much to offer in the treatment of Distemper and in this respect we are more fortunate than our conventional or allopathic colleagues in having a choice of excellent remedies according to the stage of the disease and the symptoms shown by the individual animal. If we now look at the various stages through which the disease may progress, we can examine in detail the remedies which are applicable to each:

1. Initial Stage

1. ACONITUM 30c. This is the outstanding remedy for the early stages and should be given as soon as possible when signs of inappetance or approaching disease are apparent. The expression will be anxious, and shivering or other signs of shock apparent. This remedy by itself might be capable of cutting short the development of further symptoms. It should be given at half-hourly intervals for a total of six doses.

2. FERRUM PHOS. 6x. This remedy is also useful in the early stages especially if the animal is of a sensitive or nervous disposition. Anxiety is not present. The throat is red and inflamed and there may be an accompanying nose-bleed.

3. BELLADONNA 30c. When this remedy is indicated the animal shows dilated pupils and may be excitable. There is a full bounding pulse and the skin is hot and dry.

2. Stage of Coryza with Lachrymation.

1. ARSEN. ALB. 1M. Restlessness is a keynote for the employment of this remedy. The animal sips water frequently but takes small amounts only. Symptoms are worse towards midnight. Discharges from the eyes and nose are acrid and excoriate the skin.

2. MERC. CORR. 30c. More severe lachrymation is associated with this remedy and in addition the secretions may become purulent showing as yellow blobs in the corner of the eyes. Symptoms are usually worse from sunset to sunrise.

3. PULSATILLA 30c. This remedy may be needed when discharges are catarrhal or bland and frequently profuse. Pulsatilla is especially suited to the animal which has a timid or gentle disposition.

3. Stage of Respiratory Involvement.

1. ANTIMONIUM TART. 6c. This is a useful remedy in the early coughing stage. Mucus can be heard rattling in the chest. There may be an accompanying lethargy and disinclination to move. Very little mucus is expectorated despite the presence of large amounts in the bronchial passages.

2. IPECACUANHA 30c. Frequent coughing characterises this remedy with possibly expectoration of bright red blood. There may be associated vomiting.

3. BRYONIA 30c. Breathing is difficult with obvious signs of pain over the chest wall. Abdominal breathing is evident because of pain in the pleura. The animal tends to lie on the affected side and pressure over the painful area gives relief.

4. LYCOPODIUM 30c. This is a useful remedy for lean or withered-looking subjects showing a periodicity of symptoms with aggravation in the late afternoon and early evening. It may be needed once pneumonia has set in. Another guiding symptom pointing to its indication is an independent movement of the nostrils which has nothing to do with breathing. I have found that the German Shepherd breed responds well to this remedy as a general rule.

5. PHOSPHORUS 30c. This remedy may also be needed once pneumonia has supervened. There are usually accompanying gastric symptoms such as vomition after drinking water which is rejected on becoming warm in the stomach. Certain breeds of dogs react very well to this remedy particularly the Scots Collie, Irish Setter and Whippet.

4. Stage of Gastro-Intestinal Involvement.

1. ARSEN. ALB. 1M. The patient shows acrid diarrhoea frequently blood-stained and having a cadaverous odour. Vomiting is usually present. The skin around the anus becomes excoriated. There is restlessness with frequent sips of small amounts of water. The skin is dry and harsh and symptoms become worse towards midnight.

2. MERC. CORR. 30c. Dysenteric stools of a slimy nature are associated with this remedy and may be more profuse during the night. There is severe straining at stool and the mouth may show ulcerative lesions.

3. VERATRUM ALB. 30c. Indicated when there is a watery diarrhoea forcibly expelled. There are signs of collapse or prostration with symptoms of pain prior to the passage of the stool. The animal shows resentment when the abdomen is touched.

4. BAPTISIA 30c. With this remedy, stools are dark and bloody. There is tenderness over the region of the liver and great thirst after vomiting. There is difficulty in swallowing solid food, and the animal appears sleepy and comatose.

5. CHINA OFFICINALIS 30c. A useful remedy which will restore some strength after loss of body fluid in diarrhoea. By itself it may control the diarrhoea.

6. PYROGEN 1M. This is a most important remedy in extreme cases where a high temperature accompanies a weak thready pulse. Discharges are extremely offensive and the animal has a generally putrid look. Generalised collapse is present.

5. Stage of Skin Involvement.

1. ANTIMONIUM CRUD. 6c. This is the classic remedy for the treatment of papular lesions which progress to vesicle and pustule formation. Itching is present and is worse at night.

2. ARSEN. ALB. 30c. The skin is tight and dry with flakes of dandruff. The coat becomes harsh and erect with severe itching. Symptoms become progressively worse towards midnight and heat tends to relieve.

3. SULPHUR IOD. 6c. The skin symptoms may be accompanied by enlarged throat glands when this remedy is indicated. The rash is itchy and the skin red.

6. Stage of Involvement of Nervous System.

1. GELSEMIUM 30c. The animal is generally lethargic and disinclined to move. The eyelids droop and there are indications of early paralysis. The muscles are sore to the touch.

2. BELLADONNA 1M. The most useful remedy when fits or convulsions appear. It should be given immediately one begins and repeated at half-hourly intervals for six doses. The eyes are reddened with dilated pupils and the skin is hot. The pulse is full and bounding. The animal should be kept away from light.

3. STRYCHNINUM 30c. This remedy will benefit cases of chorea. Twitchings occur in various parts especially on the face and along the back. There is a tendency to stretch the hind legs behind the body.

4. CONIUM 30c. One of the principal remedies for hind-limb paralysis. Signs of weakness first appear in the foot and ascend gradually. Ascending potencies of this remedy are generally required over a period of a few weeks.

5. CAUSTICUM 6c. Signs of paralysis may appear in other areas, e.g. the fore-leg with muscular weakness and trembling leading to an inability to stand. Before this stage appears there is a disinclination to move. Joints become stiff and may produce a creaking sound.

6. HYOSCYAMUS 30c. Brain symptoms apart from fits may arise when this remedy is needed. The head is shaken to and fro while unsteadiness is seen due to vertigo. There is inability to fix attention with the eyes, and great excitement may ensue. This usually precedes the stage of fits.

7. STRAMONIUM 30c. Vertigo is again prominent, the animal showing a tendency to fall to one side, usually the left. The patient startles easily at the least sound. Bright or glittering objects bring on an attack and for this reason the animal should be confined to a dark room.

7. Stage of Eye Involvement.
Eye complications usually take the form of keratitis or inflammation of the cornea. Ulcerations of the corneal surface also take place. Remedies which may help include the following:

1. *AURUM MET. 30c.* The bones around the eyes are painful when touched. The eyes have a reddish appearance and are generally prominent.

2. *MERC. CORR. 30c.* Corneal ulceration may require this remedy if there is an accompanying greenish pus in the inner canthus and possibly a generalised purulent conjunctivitis.

3. *SILICEA 30c.* Suitable for long-standing cases showing opacities after healing of ulceration. This remedy possesses the power of absorbing scar tissue and should be given twice weekly over a period of a few months.

4. *EUPHRASIA 6c.* Excessive lachrymation in the early stages may require this remedy. The eyelids swell and appear heavy.

5. *ACID. NIT. 30c.* A very good remedy for corneal ulcerations. There may be accompanying lesions around the mouth and anus.

6. *ARGENT. NIT. 6c.* Another very good remedy for corneal ulceration, more adapted to the requirements of the younger animal. The conjunctiva has a distinct dark pink look with a profuse purulent discharge being present. These symptoms are relieved if the animal has access to open air. If eye symptoms appear to deteriorate with the onset of abdominal lesions then Argentum Nitricum will be especially helpful.

7. *PULSATILLA 30c.* Pain in the eyes causes the animal to press the head against any suitable object. Profuse creamy discharges are usual which tend to agglutinate the eyelids. Symptoms are generally worse at night and the eyes have a fixed staring look. Sight is usually lost probably due to incipient cataract. There is great sensitivity to light.

Externally in all cases the eyes should be bathed with a 1/10 solution of *CALENDULA* and *HYPERICUM* repeated a few times each day.

If the disease is noticed in the early stages the use of potentised virus by itself may achieve spectacular results, using ascending potencies up to 50M. It is probably better, however, if the potentised virus is combined with the remedies indicated above when it can be given daily for three consecutive days.

PREVENTION OF DISTEMPER

Many owners and breeders may be unaware that a homoeopathic alternative exists to the conventional vaccine by inoculation. This takes the form of a nosode or oral vaccine which has been prepared from various specimens of killed distemper exudate and potentised to 30c. I do not wish to imply that the conventional vaccine is without merit as it does provide protection, circulating antibodies being present in the blood-stream after vaccination, and the great majority of dogs so protected will withstand challenge from virus. This method, however, is not without some danger to a small percentage of animals and cases have been recorded where some puppies have developed intractable eczema dating from the time of inoculation, and others which have developed fits as a result of protein shock.

The procedure for the homoeopathic alternative involves a course of the nosode given over a period of six months. This may seem tedious to some but the method is completely safe and without any risk of side-effects. Experiments in the U.S.A. have shown that puppies protected in this way have survived challenge from virulent distemper virus, the only reaction being a slight cough which disappeared in 48 hours.

2. INFECTIOUS CANINE HEPATITIS. RUBARTH'S DISEASE.

This virus appears to be confined to the canidae. It may appear singly or be complicated by Distemper and mortality is greater if it is thus complicated. Otherwise it frequently takes a mild form and is often missed, the severe forms being presented for treatment.

EPIZOOTIOLOGY. Foxes as well as dogs being susceptible, this species is a potent reservoir of virus and in this animal the disease manifests itself as an encephalitis. Spread of the virus takes place through the urine and unlike the Distemper virus it is not air-borne. After recovery dogs can continue to excrete the virus through their kidneys for many months, susceptible animals becoming infected by licking urine-contaminated surfaces or eating contaminated food.

CLINICAL SIGNS. The virus is infective to all ages and after an incubation period up to ten days a rise in temperature takes place which subsides after one or two days, and again rises over a period of five or six days. Mild cases may show no other symptoms. If the disease progresses, loss of appetite develops along with increased thirst. Visible mucous membranes become congested giving them a reddish-pink or brick-coloured look. Small haemorrhages may appear on these membranes. The throat becomes tender and swollen due to tonsillitis. Liver involvement is common giving rise to pain on palpation over the hepatic area. The eyes are frequently affected, conditions ranging from lachrymation to conjunctivitis accompanying serous discharges. A frequent complication is corneal opacity which gives rise to a bluish look. Small haemorrhages may occur in the skin, particularly on the abdomen, the blood becoming fluid and not clotting easily. Convalescent animals show weight loss which tends to persist even after the appetite returns to normal.

TREATMENT. The following remedies are all applicable in their own particular sphere and according to symptoms displayed.

1. ACONITUM 30c. As in other infectious diseases, the early administration of this remedy will go far to limiting its development. It should be given frequently over a few hours.

2. RHUS TOX. 6c. A very useful remedy for the stage of mucous membrane involvement showing reddish discoloration. Eyes will also benefit from this remedy.

3. PHYTOLACCA 30c. Throat symptoms should be relieved by Phytolacca, especially cases showing enlargement of neighbouring lymphatic glands.

4. MERC. IOD. RUB. 6c. This is a good remedy for throat involvement on the left side.

5. MERC. IOD. FLAV. 6c. The yellow iodine of mercury also acts on the throat but tends to favour the right side.

6. PHOSPHORUS 30c. The remedy of choice to control petechial and ecchymotic haemorrhages on the skin may also have a beneficial effect on the liver.

7. *CROTALUS HORR. 30c.* Probably the best remedy to give where stimulation of liver function is needed and haemorrhages show little tendency to clot.

8. *SILICEA 30c.* Should be given in those cases showing bluish discoloration of the eyes as it will hasten absorption of corneal oedema, which causes opacity, and prevent scar tissue formation.

9. *BERBERIS VUL. 6c.* This remedy has a beneficial action on the liver and gall bladder and also on the kidneys and its use should help prevent kidney damage due to the continued presence of the virus in these organs.

10. *HEPATITIS NOSODE 30c.* This nosode can be given along with any of the above remedies and will greatly assist the healing process. It will be of especial value in the convalescent animal which should recover weight more quickly under its influence. In this connection it can profitably be combined with a constitutional remedy such as *LYCOPODIUM 30c.*

PREVENTION OF CANINE HEPATITIS

A nosode exists and can be given either by itself or along with *CANINE DISTEMPER NOSODE.* This oral vaccine is not incorporated into the commercial Distemper nosode available and has to be purchased as a separate entity. One dose night and morning for three days should be followed by one dose per month for six months.

3. HERPES VIRUS INFECTION

This disease causes illness and death in young pups, older animals being only mildly affected.

EPIZOOTIOLOGY. Spread probably takes place through animals being congregated in over-crowded conditions and direct contact is the mode of transmission. It is not thought that air-borne spread takes place. Infected dogs can excrete the virus through nasal and oral secretions for a fortnight after infection has taken place and spread can also occur through contaminated urine. If pregnant bitches become infected, pups in utero are at risk and also in passage through the birth canal if the mother comes into contact with virus. Handling of pups at birth can also spread infection if proper cleanliness is not observed.

CLINICAL SIGNS. Pups may show signs of infection up to three weeks of age. Abdominal symptoms are the first manifestations of illness, taking the form of soft greenish stools followed by signs of general involvement such as laboured breathing and retching or vomiting. Paddling movements occur probably due to abdominal pain which causes incessant crying. It is usual for entire litters to show symptoms. In the older animal nasal discharge and difficulty in swallowing may be the only signs.

TREATMENT. A remarkable feature of this disease is the absence of fever and if pups can be quickly removed to a warm dry atmosphere in a confined space and kept well wrapped in warm material it will greatly hasten their chances of recovery. The following remedies should be on hand immediately a litter is born in case they may be needed:

1. ACONITUM 12x. Should be given as routine to all pups, two doses one hour apart.

2. ARSEN. ALB. 30c. Will help control the retching and abdominal symptoms and aid a rise in temperature.

3. CARBO VEG. 200c. Moribund pups will show a good response to this remedy. It will also help the laboured breathing by relieving air hunger.

4. ABROTANUM 1x. This remedy is well-adapted to troubles of the new-born and is worth keeping in mind. It will especially be indicated if umbilical abnormalities are present, e.g. patent urachus.

5. HERPES VIRUS NOSODE 30c. Should be given along with other remedies.

PREVENTION

HERPES VIRUS NOSODE can be prepared from infective secretions and should be administered to all pregnant bitches, giving a weekly dose during gestation. This will greatly reduce the likelihood of infected pups being born. Homoeopathic oral vaccines and nosodes have the great value of being able to cross the placental barrier because of their cellular affinity and their dependence on energy transfer.

4. PARVOVIRUS DISEASE

This is a virus infection which principally affects puppies, although older animals are also susceptible to a lesser degree. Rapid deaths can follow infection in the young animal, chiefly from dehydration and involvement of the heart muscle.

ETIOLOGY. Various viruses have been implicated with names such as CPV (parvo-like) and CCV (corona-like). The virus is believed to be closely related to that which causes enteritis in mink and to that causing feline panleucopenia. Stress is an added factor which makes the animal more susceptible.

CLINICAL SIGNS. Typically the disease has a sudden onset, with the patient showing signs of depression. Vomiting and diarrhoea soon set in, the faeces being watery, extremely foul-smelling and having an orange-yellow colour. Blood may be present both in the stomach contents and the faeces. Dehydration is marked especially in puppies. The temperature may be only slightly raised and as often as not is normal. The mouth may show small vesicles which, on rupturing, leave a raw bleeding surface.

DIAGNOSIS. This is based on clinical signs, although laboratory tests will show which particular virus is responsible. Blood tests show a deficiency of white blood-cells.

TREATMENT. If disease is suspected, the following remedies should be considered:

1. ACONITUM 30c. Should be given as soon as possible, one dose every hour for four doses. This remedy will also have a most beneficial effect on any dog which the owner or attendant may think has been subjected to stress in any form.

2. PHOSPHORUS 30c. This is the remedy of choice to control gastric symptoms. One dose should be given every hour for four doses and this usually succeeds in allaying vomiting. It also helps control any bleeding from the stomach.

3. ARSEN. ALB. 30c. This remedy is the main one to control diarrhoea in the acute stages, and again frequent doses are necessary.

4. IRIS VERSICOLOR 30c. This is a useful remedy to follow after acute symptoms have been controlled by the previous remedies.

5. CROTALUS HORR. 30c. If there is considerable blood being lost in the faeces it may be necessary to employ this remedy in addition to those already mentioned. It is one of the main antihaemorrhagic remedies we have and frequent doses are advisable.

PREVENTION

A homoeopathic oral vaccine exists based on the causative virus and the usual recommendation is as follows:

One dose should be given night and morning for three days followed by one per month for six months. This nosode can be given to pups of an early age, e.g. two to three weeks and thereby offers an advantage over conventional vaccines. It is entirely safe and without any side effects. Experience in practice has shown that this nosode has given consistently good results and no breakdowns have been reported. The oral vaccine can also be used to supplement the remedies outlined and will aid their action.

Protozoal Infections

1. BABESIASIS

This vector-borne disease is also known as biliary fever and malignant jaundice.

ETIOLOGY. B. Canis is the commonest of the various species of babesia which are implicated. The disease is transmitted by a dog tick which acts as intermediate host.

CLINICAL SIGNS. There may be an incubation period up to 4 or 5 weeks which is followed by a rise in temperature with increased heart and respiration rates. Anaemia becomes progresively apparent, shown in the pallor of visible mucous membranes. Anorexia and depression set in along with symptoms of jaundice implying liver involvement which in turn leads to ascites.

TREATMENT. The chief remedies to be considered are as follows:

1. ACONITUM 12x. For the early feverish state and should be given as early as possible.

2. CROTALUS HORR. 30c. Probably the most important remedy to be considered in bilious states with haemorrhagic complications. The presence of icteric changes will further determine its use. It may have to be given frequently during any acute phase.

3. PHOSPHORUS 30c. This is another useful remedy to consider in milder cases. It also has a beneficial action on the liver and will control the tendency to small haemorrhages.

4. CHINA OFFICINALIS 30c. Possesses the power of restoring loss of body-fluid, and should always be used in conjunction with other remedies.

5. TRINITROTOLUENE 30c. This substance in the crude state possesses the ability to destroy red blood cells with the attendant loss of haemoglobin. It should therefore be considered in biliary fever as its symptom picture covers many of the manifestations of this disease.

2. TOXOPLASMOSIS

This disease is caused by a protozoan organism called Toxoplasma gondii which becomes intracellular causing a pneumonia-like disease with abdominal and central nervous system complications.

CLINICAL SIGNS. These vary according to the tissues or organs involved and the age of the affected animal, pups showing more severe symptoms than older dogs. The initial febrile stage ushers in pneumonia with coughing. Discharges of muco-purulent material may be seen from both the nose and eyes. An abdominal form also occurs producing gastro-enteritis, the animal resenting pressure over the stomach area. The central nervous system is commonly affected producing signs of inco-ordination, fits and various degrees of paralysis. The ocular discharges are dependent on lesions such as iritis and keratitis.

TREATMENT

1. ACONITUM 12x. Should be given at the first signs of febrile disturbance.

2. PHOSPHORUS 30c. One of the main remedies to be considered in pneumonia, the animal showing nasal discharge which may be rust-coloured. If thirst is present vomiting takes place when the stomach contents become warm after drinking.

3. ARSENICUM ALB. 1M. The best remedy for the gastro-intestinal form. The coat will be harsh and dry and the animal usually seeks warmth, symptoms being worse towards midnight.

4. MERC. CORR. 30c. A good remedy for the treatment of eye conditions showing muco-purulent discharges. There may also be slimy, blood-stained diarrhoea.

5. BELLADONNA 1M. Probably the most useful remedy for animals which develop fits.

6. CONIUM 30c. If signs of paresis or early paralysis in the hind-quarters develop, this remedy is indicated.

7. STRYCHNINUM 200c. Muscular twitchings and St. Vitus Dance will be helped by this remedy.

Diseases of Puppyhood

Apart from congenital abnormalities and surgical interferences which do not concern us here, the following conditions are worthy of note:

1. NUTRITIONAL ANAEMIA

This may appear when pups are about two weeks old and is manifested by paleness of visible mucous membranes and progressive weakness. Remedies which are likely to help are *TRINITROTOLUENE 30c*, *FERRUM IOD. 6c* and *CHINA 30c*. Administration of *TRINITRO-TOLUENE* to the pregnant bitch in the last two weeks of gestation may help prevent the occurrence of anaemia in the offspring.

2. RICKETS

This disease is not uncommon in 'winter' litters, but much less so in those pups born in the spring or early summer. Affected pups show swelling of joints and lameness which may progress to bending of the long bones of the limbs and curvature of the thoracic cage. Apart from the feeding of Vit. D the following remedies will be of great value:

1. CALC. CARB. 30c. This remedy is suitable for 'soft' fat puppies especially those of the brachycephalic breeds. It should be given weekly for two months, and will greatly assist the calcium metabolism.

2. CALC. PHOS. 30c. This acts in the same way as the previous remedy but is more suitable for leaner puppies, and overall is probably more effective in the developing animal, because of its phosphorus content.

3. HYPERTROPHIC OSTEODYSTROPHY

This condition occurs in older pups up to the time of weaning and after, and is characterised by swellings at the end of the long bones. These are acutely painful and the animal is unwilling to walk any distance. There is constitutional involvement manifested by a high temperature. Skin symptoms may also occur, such as scurvy-like lesions. Homoeopathy is fortunate in possessing certain remedies which may have a beneficial effect, as conventional medicine can do little to help. Chief among those are the following:

1. CALC. FLUOR. 30c. This is a good general remedy for bone conditions and will act on periosteal and joint swellings. It should not be repeated too often.

2. HECLA LAVA 12c. This remedy also has a specific action on bones, particularly bony swellings and exostoses appearing on the upper jaw.

3. RUTA GRAV. 6c. A useful remedy for the initial inflammatory involvement of the periosteum of bone. It will quickly relieve pain and prevent further deterioration.

4. ANGUSTURA VERA 30c. A good remedy for stiffness and heaviness of limbs showing an almost paralysed appearance. Some bones may show necrosis and caries.

5. CALC. PHOS. 30c. A useful remedy for promoting health in the musculo-skeletal system of the growing animal.

4. DISTEMPER

This disease can be transmitted via the mother when weak puppies are likely to be born and ultimately show disease symptoms. The classical signs of distemper are the same in the pup as in the older dog and treatment should follow the same lines (see under Distemper in Virus Diseases). Administration of *DISTEMPERINUM 30c* to the pregnant bitch will reduce the likelihood of the disease being transmitted to the unborn pup.

5. HEPATITIS

This can occur in the young pup and sometimes gives no indication of its presence, disease being suspected by acute loss of condition in otherwise healthy pups with continual crying for anything up to 18 hours. *HEPATITIS NOSODE* can be combined with remedies such as *PHOSPHORUS 30c* and *LYCOPODIUM 30c*, both of which exert a beneficial action on the liver. Accompanying jaundice may be controlled by *CHELIDONIUM 30c* or *CROTALUS HORR. 30c*.

6. NEONATAL SEPTICAEMIA

Symptoms of this trouble, which is due mainly to species of Streptococcus, are similar to those of other infectious diseases in the very young animal, viz. acute loss of condition in normally healthy animals which then die quickly. Abdominal pain is present and the abdomen is often hard and drum-like. Prevention lies in treating the bitch with *STREPTOCOCCUS 30c* using a compound nosode. Other organisms which produce septicaemia in the young pup are Pseudomonas species and strains of E. Coli. The appropriate nosode in each case should be used for prevention. Remedies which may help in treating less severe forms of septicaemia are *ECHINACEA* and *PYROGEN*, the former in low potency and the latter in high.

7. PUSTULAR DERMATITIS

This condition appears as a pimply or pustular rash particularly on the head, involving the eyes and lips. Secondary infection leads to suppurative swelling of neighbouring lymphatic glands. Remedies which are likely to help are *HEPAR SULPH. 30c* which will clear the suppurative process and prevent spread, *ANTIMONIUM CRUD. 6c* which is useful for the papular stage and *VARIOLINUM* which, given early, will prevent development of the lesion to the pustular and scab stages. *RHUS TOX. 6c* is a useful remedy if the lesions are accompanied by erythema and severe itching. The intercurrent use of *STAPHYLOCOCCUS 30c* is also helpful and will assist the action of other remedies.

Materia Medica

Abies Canadensis. Hemlock Spruce. N.O. Coniferae.
The Ø is made from the fresh bark and young buds.

This plant has an affinity for mucous membranes generally and that of the stomach in particular, producing a catarrhal gastritis. Impairment of liver function occurs leading to flatulence and deficient bile-flow. Appetite is increased and hunger may be ravenous. It is chiefly used as a digestive remedy.

Abrotanum. Southernwood. N.O. Compositae.
Tincture of fresh leaves.

This plant produces wasting of muscles of lower limbs and is used for animals showing this weakness. A prominent guiding symptom in the young animal is umbilical oozing of fluid. It is one of the remedies used to control worm infestation in young animals and also has a reputation in certain forms of acute arthritis where overall symptoms agree.

Absinthium. Wormwood.
Infusions of active principle.

The effect on the system of this substance is to produce a picture of confusion and convulsions preceded by trembling of muscles. There is a marked action on the central nervous system causing the patient to fall backwards. The pupils of the eye may show unequal dilation. It is one of the main remedies used in practice to control epileptiform seizures and fits of varying kinds.

Acidum Salicylicum. Salicylic Acid.
Trituration of powder.

This acid has an action on joints, producing swellings and in some cases caries of bone. Gastric symptoms, e.g. bleeding, are also prominent in its provings. Homoeopathically indicated in the treatment of rheumatic and osteo-arthritic conditions and idiopathic gastric bleeding.

Aconitum Napellus. Monkshood. N.O. Ranunculaceae.
In the preparation of the Ø the entire plant is used as all parts contain aconitine the active principle.

This plant has an affinity for serous membranes and muscular tissues leading to functional disturbances. There is sudden involvement and tension in all parts. This remedy should be used in the early stages of all feverish conditions where there is sudden appearance of symptoms which may also show an aggravation when any extreme of temperature takes place. Predisposing factors which may produce a drug picture calling for Aconitum include shock, operation and exposure to cold dry winds, or dry heat. It could be of use in puerperal conditions showing sudden involvement with peritoneal complications.

Actaea Racemosa. Black Snake Root. Also referred to as Cimicifuga Racemosa. N.O. Ranunculaceae.
Trituration of its resin.

This plant resin has a wide range of action on various body systems, chief among which are the female genital and the articular, leading to disturbances of the uterus in particular and small joint arthritis. Muscular pains are evident, affection of cervical vertebrae being evidenced by stiffening of neck muscles.

Adonis Vernalis. Pheasant's Eye. N.O. Ranunculaceae.
Infusion of fresh plant.

The main action of the remedy which concerns us in veterinary practice is its cardial action which becomes weak leading to dropsy and scanty output of urine. It is one of the main remedies used in valvular disease and difficult respiration dependent on pulmonary congestion.

Aesculus Hippocastanum. Horse Chestnut. N.O. Sapindaceae.
The Ø is prepared from the fruit with capsule.

The main affinity of this plant is with the lower bowel, producing a state of venous congestion. There is a general slowing down of the digestive and circulatory systems, the liver and portal action becoming sluggish. This is associated with a tendency to dry stools. It is a useful remedy in hepatic conditions with venous congestion affecting the general circulation and it also has a place in the treatment of congestive chest conditions.

171

Agaricus Muscarius. Fly Agaric. N.O. Fungi.
The Ø is prepared from the fresh fungus.

Muscarin is the best known toxic compound of several which are found in this fungus. Symptoms of poisoning are generally delayed from anything up to twelve hours after ingestion. The main sphere of action is on the central nervous system producing a state of vertigo and delirium followed by sleepiness. There are four recognised stages of cerebral excitement, viz: 1. Slight stimulation. 2. Intoxication with mental excitement accompanied by twitching. 3. Delirium. 4. Depression with soporific tendency. These actions determine its use in certain conditions affecting the central nervous system, e.g. cerebro-cortical necrosis and meningitis, which may accompany severe attacks of hypomagnesaemia. Tympanitic conditions with flatus may respond favourably, while it also has a place as a rheumatic remedy and in the treatment of some forms of muscular cramp.

Agnus Castus. Chaste Tree. N.O. Verbenaceae.
Tincture of ripe berries.

One of the principal spheres of action relating to this plant is the sexual system, where it produces a lowering or depression of functions with accompanying debility. In the male there may be induration and swelling of testicles and in the female sterility has been reported.

Aletris Farinosa. Star Grass. N.O. Haemodoraceae.
The Ø is prepared from the root.

This plant has an affinity with the female genital tract, especially the uterus and is used mainly as an anti-abortion remedy and in the treatment of uterine discharges and also in silent heat in animals which may show an accompanying loss of appetite.

Allium Cepa. Onion. N.O. Liliaceae.
The Ø is prepared from the whole plant.

A picture of coryza with acrid nasal discharge and symptoms of laryngeal discomfort is associated with this plant. It could be indicated in the early stages of most catarrhal conditions producing the typical coryza.

Alumen. Potash Alum.
Trituration of the pure crystals.

Indicated in affections of arms and in conditions affecting mucous membranes of various body systems, producing dryness; affections of the central nervous system are also common, resulting in varying degrees of paralysis.

Ammonium Carbonicum. Ammonium Carbonate.
This salt is used as a solution in distilled water from which the potencies are prepared.

It is primarily used in respiratory affections especially when there is an accompanying swelling of associated lymph glands. Emphysema, pulmonary oedema and fog fever are thoracic conditions which may be helped by this remedy. It is also useful in digestive upsets.

Ammonium Causticum. Hydrate of Ammonia.
Potencies are again prepared from a solution in distilled water.

This salt has a similar but more pronounced action on mucous membranes to that of the carbonate, producing ulcerations on these surfaces. It is also a powerful cardiac stimulant. Mucosal disease may call for its use, also respiratory conditions showing severe involvement of the lungs. There is usually an excess of mucus with a moist cough when this remedy is indicated.

Angustura Vera. N.O. Rutaceae.
Trituration of tree bark.

Bones and muscles come prominently into consideration when this plant is specified. Stiffness and limb pains of varying degree are prominent along with exostosis. Mild paralysis of legs has been noted. The action on bones may lead on to caries with possible fractures developing.

Anthracinum. Anthrax Poison.
The Ø is prepared from affected tissue or culture dissolved in alcohol.

This nosode is indicated in the treatment of eruptive skin diseases which are characterised by boil-like swellings. Cellular tissue becomes indurated and swelling of associated lymph glands takes place. The characteristic lesion assumes the form of a hard swelling with a necrotic centre and surrounded by a blackened rim. It has proved useful in the treatment of septic bites.

Antimonium Arsenicosum. Arsenite of Antimony.
Potencies are prepared from trituration of the dried salt dissolved in distilled water or alcohol.

This salt possesses a selective action on the lungs especially the upper left area and is used mainly in the treatment of emphysema and long-standing pneumonias. Coughing, if present, is worse on eating and the animal prefers to stand rather than lie down.

Antimonium Crudum. Sulphide of Antimony.
Potencies prepared from trituration of the dried salt.

This substance exerts a strong influence on the stomach and skin, producing conditions which are aggravated by heat. Any vesicular skin condition should be influenced favourably.

Antimonium Tartaricum. Tartar Emetic. Tartrate of Antimony and Potash.
Trituration of the dried salt is the source of potencies.

Respiratory symptoms predominate with this drug, affections being accompanied by the production of excess mucus, although expectoration is difficult. The main action being on the respiratory system, we should expect this remedy to be beneficial in conditions such as broncho-pneumonia and pulmonary oedema. Ailments requiring this remedy frequently show an accompanying drowsiness and lack of thirst. In pneumonic states, the edges of the eyes may be covered with mucus.

Apis Mellifica. Bee Venom.
The Ø is prepared from the entire insect and also from the venom diluted with alcohol.

The poison of the bee acts on cellular tissue causing oedema and swelling. The production of oedema anywhere in the system may lead to a variety of acute and chronic conditions. Considering the well-documented evidence of its sphere of action affecting all tissues and mucous membranes, we should consider this remedy in conditions showing oedematous swellings. Synovial swellings of joints may respond to its use. Respiratory conditions showing an excess of pulmonary fluid or oedema, e.g. fog fever, have been treated successfully with this remedy, while it has also been used to good effect in the treatment of cystic ovaries. All ailments are aggravated by heat and are thirstless.

174

Apocynum Cannabinum. Indian Hemp. N.O Apocynaceae.
Infusions of the fresh plant.

This substance produces disturbance of gastric function along with affection of heart muscle leading to a slowing of its action. There is also a marked action on the uro-genital system producing diuresis and uterine bleeding. The patient requiring this remedy may present symptoms of drowsiness or stupor. Upper respiratory symptoms are common, e.g. nasal secretions of yellowish mucus.

Apomorphinum.
This is one of the alkaloids of morphine and has a profound action on the vomiting centre of the brain producing several emissis preceded by increased secretion of saliva and mucous. Pupils become dilated. It is used in veterinary practice to produce complete emptying of stomach contents after suspected poisoning or ingestion of foreign matter, and homoeopathically to control prolonged and severe vomiting.

Argentum Nitricum. Silver Nitrate.
This remedy is prepared by trituration of the salt and subsequent dissolving in alcohol or distilled water.

It produces inco-ordination of movement causing trembling in various parts. It has an irritant effect on mucous membranes producing a free-flowing muco-purulent discharge. Red blood cells are affected, anaemia being caused by their destruction. Its sphere of action makes it a useful remedy in eye conditions.

Arnica Montana. Leopard's Bane. N.O. Compositae.
The Ø is prepared from the whole fresh plant.

The action of this plant upon the system is practically synonymous with a state resulting from injuries or blows. It is known as the 'Fall Herb' and is used mainly for wounds and injuries where the skin remains unbroken. It has a marked affinity with blood-vessels leading to dilation, stasis and increased permeability. Thus various types of haemorrhage can occur. It reduces shock when given in potency and should be given routinely before and after surgical interference when it will also help control bleeding. Given after parturition, it will hasten recovery of bruised tissue. While given during pregnancy at regular intervals, it will help promote normal easy parturition.

Arsenicum Album. Arsenic Trioxide.
This remedy is prepared by trituration and subsequent dilution.

It is a deep-acting remedy and acts on every tissue of the body and its characteristic and definite symptoms make its use certain in many ailments. Discharges are acrid and burning and symptoms are relieved by heat. It is of use in many skin conditions associated with dryness, scaliness and itching. Coli-bacillosis and coccidiosis are conditions which may call for its use. It could also have a role to play in some forms of pneumonia when the patient may show a desire for small quantities of water and symptoms become worse towards midnight.

Arsenicum Iodatum. Iodide of Arsenic.
Potencies are prepared from the triturated salt dissolved in distilled water.

When discharges are persistently irritating and corrosive, this remedy may prove more beneficial than *ARSEN. ALB*. The mucous membranes become red, swollen and oedematous, especially in the respiratory sphere. This remedy is frequently called for in bronchial and pneumonic conditions which are at the convalescent stage or in those ailments which have not responded satisfactorily to seemingly indicated remedies.

Atropinum. An Alkaloid of Belladonna.
This alkaloid produces some of the effects of Belladonna itself but acts more particularly on the eyes, causing dilation the of pupils and mucous membranes generally which become extremely dry. It could be indicated where overall symptoms of Belladonna are not well-defined.

Baptisia Tinctoria. Wild Indigo. N.O. Leguminosae.
The Ø is prepared from fresh root and bark.

The symptoms produced by this plant relate mainly to septicaemic conditions producing prostration and weakness. Low-grade fevers and great muscular lethargy are present in the symptomatology. All secretions and discharges are very offensive. Profuse salivation occurs, together with ulceration of the gums, which become discoloured. Tonsils and throat are dark red and stools tend to be dysenteric. It should be remembered as a possibly useful remedy in some forms of enteritis when other symptoms agree.

Baryta Carbonica. Barium Carbonate.
Potencies are prepared from trituration of the salt dissolved in distilled water.

The action of this salt produces symptoms and conditions more usually seen in old and very young subjects and should be remembered as a useful remedy for certain conditions affecting the respiratory system especially.

Baryta Muriatica. Barium Chloride.
Solution of salt in distilled water.

This salt produces periodic attacks of convulsions with spastic involvement of limbs. Ear discharges appear which are offensive and the parotid salivary glands become swollen. Induration of abdominal glands develops including the pancreas. It is indicated in many instances of ear canker and also in animals which show a tendency to develop glandular swellings along with the characteristic involvement of the nervous system.

Belladonna. Deadly Nightshade. N.O. Solanaceae.
The Ø is prepared from the whole plant at flowering.

This plant produces a profound action on every part of the central nervous system, causing a state of excitement and active congestion. The effect also on the skin, glands and vascular system is constant and specific. One of the main guiding symptoms in prescribing is the presence of a full bounding pulse in any feverish condition which may or may not accompany excitable states. Another guiding symptom is dilation of pupils.

Bellis Perennis. Daisy. N.O. Compositae.
The Ø is prepared from the whole fresh plant.

The main action of this little flower is on the muscular tissues of blood vessels producing a state of venous congestion. Systemic muscles become heavy, leading to a halting type of gait suggestive of pain. This is a useful remedy to aid recovery of tissues injured during cutting or after operation. Sprains and bruises in general come within its sphere of action and it should be kept in mind as an adjunct remedy along with *ARNICA*. Given post-partum it will hasten resolution of bruised tissue and enable the pelvic area to recover tone in a very short time.

Benzoicum Acidum. Benzoic Acid.
Potencies are prepared from gum benzoin which is triturated and dissolved in alcohol.

The most outstanding feature of this remedy relates to the urinary system, producing changes in the colour and odour of the urine, which becomes dark red and aromatic with uric acid deposits. It may have a place in the treatment of some kidney and bladder conditions.

Berberis Vulgaris. Barberry. N.O. Berberidaceae.
The Ø is prepared from the bark of the root.

This shrub of wide distribution has an affinity with most tissues. Symptoms which it produces are liable to alternate violently, e.g. feverish conditions with thirst can quickly give way to prostration without any desire for water. It acts forcibly on the venous system producing especially pelvic engorgements. The chief ailments which come within its sphere of action are those connected with the liver and kidneys, leading to catarrhal inflammation of bile ducts and kidney pelvis. Jaundice frequently attends such conditions. Haematuria and cystitis may occur. In all these conditions there is an accompanying sacral weakness and tenderness over the loins.

Beryllium. The Metal.
Trituration and subsequent dissolving in alcohol produces the tincture from which the potencies are prepared.

This remedy is used mainly in respiratory conditions where the leading symptom is difficult breathing on slight exertion and which is out of proportion to clinical findings. Coughing and emphysema are usually present. This is a useful remedy in virus pneumonia, both acute and chronic forms, where symptoms are few while the animal is resting, but become pronounced on movement. It is a deep-acting remedy and should not be used below 30c potency.

Borax. Sodium Biborate.
Potencies are prepared from trituration of the salt dissolved in distilled water.

This salt produces gastro-intestinal irritation with mouth symptoms of salivation and ulceration. With most complaints there is fear of downward motion. The specific action of this substance on the epithelium of the mouth, tongue and buccal mucosa determines its use as a remedy which will control such conditions as vesicular stomatitis and allied diseases, e.g. mucosal disease.

Bothrops Lanceolatus. Yellow Viper.
Potencies are prepared from solution of the venom in glycerine.

This poison is associated with haemorrhages and subsequent rapid coagulation of blood. Septic involvement takes place as a rule and this is, therefore, a useful remedy in septic states showing haemorrhagic tendencies. Gangrenous conditions of the skin may respond to it.

Bromium. Bromine. The Element.
Potencies are prepared from solutions in distilled water.

Bromine is found in combinations with iodine in the ash when seaweed is burned, and also in sea water. It acts chiefly on the mucous membrane of the respiratory tract, especially the upper trachea, causing laryngeal spasm. This is a useful remedy for a croup-like cough accompanied by rattling of mucus. Its indication in respiratory ailments is related to symptoms being aggravated on inspiration. It may be of use also in those conditions which arise from over-exposure to heat.

Bryonia Alba. White Bryony. Wild Hop. N.O. Cucurbitaceae.
The Ø is prepared from the root before flowering takes place.

This important plant produces a glucoside which is capable of bringing on severe purgation. The plant itself exerts its main action on epithelial tissues and serous and synovial membranes. Some mucous surfaces are also affected, producing an inflammatory response resulting in a fibrinous or serous exudate. This in turn leads to dryness of the affected tissue with later effusions into synovial cavities. Movement of the parts is interfered with and this leads to one of the main indications for its use, viz. all symptoms are worse from movement, the animal preferring to lie still. Pressure over affected areas relieves symptoms. This remedy may be extremely useful in treating the many respiratory conditions met with, especially pleurisy where the above symptom picture is seen.

Bufo. The Toad. N.O. Buforidae. Solution of Poison.
This remedy is used in states of cerebral excitement sometimes severe enough to precipitate epilepsy. Dropsical states also develop. Has also been used in cases of exaggerated sexual impulses especially in the male.

Cactus Grandiflorus. Night-Blooming Cereus. N.O. Cactaceae.
The Ø is prepared from young stems and flowers.
   The active principle of this plant acts on circular muscle fibres and has a marked affinity for the cardio-vascular system. It is mainly confined to the treatment of valvular disease, but it may also be of service in some conditions showing a haemorrhagic tendency.

Calcarea Carbonica. Carbonate of Lime.
Trituration of the salt in alcohol or weak acid produces the solution from which potencies are prepared. The crude substance is found in the middle layer of the oyster shell.
   This calcareous substance produces a lack of tone and muscular weakness with muscle spasm affecting both voluntary and involuntary muscles. Calcium is excreted quickly from the system and the intake of calcium salts does not ensure against conditions which may need the element prepared in the homoeopathic manner. *CALC. CARB.* is a strong constitutional remedy causing impaired nutrition, and animals which need potentised calcium show a tendency to eat strange objects. It is of value in the treatment of skeletal disorders of young animals and in the older animal suffering from osteomalacia.

Calcarea Fluorica. Fluorspar. Fluoride of Lime.
Potencies are prepared from trituration of the salt with subsequent dilution in distilled water.
   Crystals of this substance are found in the Haversian canals of bone. This increases the hardness, but in excess produces brittleness. It also occurs in tooth enamel and in the epidermis of the skin. Affinity with all these tissues may lead to the establishment of exostoses and glandular enlargements. It is in addition a powerful vascular remedy. The special sphere of action of this remedy lies in its relation to bone lesions especially exostoses. Both actinomycosis and actinobacillosis may benefit from its use.

Calcarea Iodata. Iodide of Lime.
Solution of salt in distilled water.

This remedy is used in cases of hardening of tissue, especially glands and tonsils. The thyroid gland is also affected and occasionally the thymus as well.

Calcarea Phosphorica. Phosphate of Lime.
Potencies are prepared from trituration and subsequent dilution, from adding dilute phosphoric acid to lime water.

This salt has an affinity with tissues which are concerned with growth and the repair of cells. Assimilation may be difficult because of impaired nutrition and delayed development. Brittleness of bone is a common feature. This is a remedy of special value in the treatment of musculo-skeletal disorders of young stock.

Calc. Renalis Phos. and Calc. Renalis Uric.
These two salts are indicated in cases of lithiasis due to the presence of stones of the respective substances. They aid the action of remedies such as *BERBERIS* and *HYDRANGEA* and *THLASPI* and can be used along with them.

Calendula Officinalis. Marigold. N.O. Compositae.
The Ø is prepared from leaves and flowers.
Applied locally to open wounds and indolent ulcers, this remedy will be found to be one of the most reliable healing agents we have. It will rapidly bring about resolution of tissue promoting healthy granulation. It should be used as a 1/10 dilution in warm water. It is helpful in treating contused wounds of the eyes and it can be combined with *HYPERICUM* when treating open wounds involving damage to nerves.

Camphora. Camphor. N.O. Lauraceae.
Potencies are prepared from a solution of the gum in rectified spirit.

This substance produces a state of collapse with weakness and failing pulse. There is icy coldness of the entire body. It has a marked relationship to muscles and fasciae. Any form of enteritis showing exhaustion and collapse may require this remedy. It may be needed in disease caused by salmonella species.

Cannabis Sativa. American Hemp. N.O. Cannabinaceae.
The Ø is prepared from the flowering tops of the plant.

This plant affects particularly the urinary, sexual and respiratory systems, conditions being accompanied by great fatigue. There is a tendency to pneumonia, pericarditis and retention of urine; this may lead to cystitis and a mucoid blood-stained urine.

Cantharis. Spanish Fly.
The Ø is prepared by trituration of the insect with subsequent dilution in alcohol.

The poisonous substances contained in this insect attack particularly the urinary and sexual organs setting up violent inflammation. The skin is also markedly affected, a severe vesicular rash developing with intense itching. This is a valuable remedy in nephritis and cystitis typified by frequent attempts at urination, the urine itself containing blood as a rule. It may be indicated in certain post-partum inflammations and burning vesicular eczemas.

Carbo Vegetabilis. Vegetable Charcoal.
Potencies are prepared by trituration and subsequent dilution in alcohol.

Various tissues of the body have a marked affinity with this substance. The circulatory system is particularly affected leading to lack of oxygenation with a corresponding increase of carbon dioxide in the blood and tissues. This in turn leads to a lack of resistance to infections and to haemorrhages of dark blood which does not readily coagulate. Coldness of the body surface supervenes. When potentised, this is a very useful remedy in all cases of collapse. Pulmonary congestions will benefit and it restores warmth and strength in cases of circulatory weakness. It acts more on the venous than on the arterial circulation.

Carduus Marianus. St. Mary's Thistle. N.O. Compositae.
Trituration of seeds dissolved in spirits.

This remedy is indicated in disorders arising from inefficiency of liver function. The action of the liver indicates its main use in veterinary practice. Cirrhotic conditions with accompanying dropsy respond well.

Caulophyllum. Blue Cohosh. N.O. Berberidaceae.
The Ø is prepared from trituration of the root dissolved in alcohol.

This plant produces pathological states related to the female genital system. Extraordinary rigidity of the *os uteri* is set up leading to difficulties at parturition. Early abortions may occur due to uterine debility. These may be accompanied by fever and thirst. There is a tendency to retention of afterbirth with possible bleeding from the uterus. In potentised form this remedy will revive labour pains and could be used as an alternative to pituitrin injections once the *os* is open. It will be found useful in ringwomb and also in cases of uterine twist or displacement. In these cases it should be given frequently for three or four doses, e.g. hourly intervals. In animals which have had previous miscarriages it will help in establishing a normal pregnancy while post-partum it is one of the remedies to be considered for retained afterbirth.

Causticum. Potassium Hydroxide.
This substance is prepared by the distillation of a mixture of equal parts of slaked lime and potassium bisulphate.

The main affinity is with the neuro-muscular system producing weakness and paresis of both types of muscle. Symptoms are aggravated by going from a cold atmosphere to a warm one. It may be of use in bronchitic conditions of older animals and in those which develop small sessile warts. It appears to have an antidotal effect in cases of lead poisoning and could be used in this connection as an adjunct to versenate injections.

Ceanothus Americanus. New Jersey Tea. N.O. Rhamnaceae.
Tincture of fresh leaves.

Splenic conditions in general come within the range of this remedy. Tenderness of the spleen may be evident. In the female, whitish vaginal discharges may arise. Chiefly used for conditions where it is thought that the spleen is involved.

Chelidonium. Greater Celandine. N.O. Papaveraceae.
The Ø is prepared from the whole plant, fresh at the time of flowering.

A specific action on the liver is produced by this plant. There is general lethargy and indisposition. The tongue is usually coated a dirty yellow and signs of jaundice may be seen in other visible mucous membranes. The liver is constantly upset with the production of clay-coloured stools. Because of its marked hepatic action it should be remembered when dealing with disturbances associated with a sluggish liver action. It may be of use in photosensitisation if signs of jaundice occur.

Chimaphilla Umbellata. Ground Holly. N.O. Ericaceae.
The Ø is prepared from the fresh plant.

The active principle of this plant produces a marked action on the kidneys and genital system of both sexes. In the eyes, cataracts may develop. The urine is mucoid and blood-stained. Enlargement of the prostate gland may develop while in the female mammary tumours and atrophy have both been recorded.

Chininum Sulphuricum. Sulphate of Quinine.
Trituration of salt dissolved in alcohol.

This salt closely resembles the action of *CHINA* and should be remembered as a useful remedy in cases of debility due to loss of essential fluids. It affects the ear, producing pain over the area and excessive secretion of wax. Conditions calling for its use tend to recur after apparent or real remissions. Septic conditions of the dog, following bites or injuries respond well and thereby reduce the likelihood of future tissue involvement of a septic nature.

Chionanthus Virginica. Fringe Tree.
Tincture of bark.

This remedy is indicated in sluggish states of the liver including early cases of cirrhosis, accompanying a generalised loss of condition and, in extreme cases, emaciation. The stools produced are clay-coloured and there may be jaundice and highly-coloured urine.

Cicuta Virosa. Water Hemlock. N.O. Umbelliferae.
The Ø is prepared from the fresh root at the time of flowering.

The central nervous system is principally affected by this plant, spasmodic affections occurring. A characteristic feature is the head and neck twisted to one side accompanied by violence of one kind or another. Aggravation occurs from jarring or sudden movement. The general balance becomes upset and there is a tendency to fall to one side while the head and spine bend backwards. Various conditions of the brain and spinal cord may benefit from this remedy, e.g. cerebro-cortical necrosis.

Cinchona Officinalis. China Officinalis. Peruvian Bark. N.O. Rubiaceae.
The Ø is prepared from the dried bark dissolved in alcohol.

This plant is commonly referred to as 'China' and is the source of quinine. Large doses tend to produce toxic changes, e.g. nervous sensitivity, impaired leucocyte formation, haemorrhages, fever and diarrhoea. Weakness ensues from loss of body fluids. This remedy should be considered when an animal is suffering from debility or exhaustion after fluid loss, e.g. severe diarrhoea or haemorrhage. It is seldom indicated in the earlier stages of acute disease.

Cineraria Maritima. Dusty Miller. N.O. Compositae.
The Ø is prepared from the whole fresh plant.

The active principle is used mainly as an external application in eye conditions. The Ø should be diluted 1/10.

Cinnabaris. Mercuric Sulphide.
Trituration of salt dissolved in alcohol.

The action of this substance relates mainly to the genito-urinary sphere where conditions such as albuminuria and balanitis tend to occur. Warts develop in the inguinal area. Eye conditions are also common such as blepharitis and ophthalmia with purulent discharge. Sometimes the ear is affected, producing a dry itching condition with scurf around the pinna. Chiefly used in practice where other mercurial remedies have given less than satisfactory results.

Cobaltum. The Metal. Cobaltum Chloridum. The Salt.
Both these remedies are used mainly in the 30c potency in the treatment of cobalt deficiency and give good results over a period of a few weeks.

Cocculus. Indian Cockle. N.O. Menispermaceae.
The Ø is prepared from powdered seeds which contain an alkaloid – pectoxin.

The active principle produces spasmodic and paretic affections deriving from the CNS (Cerebrum), not the spinal cord. There is a strong tendency to vomit due to the action on the vomiting centre which appears to be dependent on movement. Mainly used in travel sickness where symptoms agree.

Coccus Cacti. Cochineal.
The Ø is prepared from the dried bodies of the female insects.

This substance has an affinity for mucous membranes producing catarrhal inflammation. Viscid mucus accumulates in the air passages leading to difficulty in expectoration and spasmodic coughing. Dysuria is common, the urine being scanty and leaving a reddish deposit on standing. It is mainly used in affections of the respiratory and urinary systems.

Colchicum Autumnale. Meadow Saffron. N.O. Liliaceae.
The Ø is prepared from the bulb.

This plant affects muscular tissues, periosteum and synovial membranes of joints. It possesses also an anti-allergic and anti-inflammatory action which interferes with the natural recuperative powers of the body. Illnesses which may require this remedy are usually acute and severe, accompanied frequently by effusions in the small joints. Autumnal diarrhoea and dysentery may also be helped, the latter accompanied by tympany and tenesmus. One of its guiding symptoms is aversion to food, while complaints requiring it are generally worse from movement.

Colocynthis. Bitter Cucumber. N.O. Cucurbitaceae.
The Ø is prepared from the fruit and contains a glucoside — colocynthin.

This plant is purgative and causes violent inflammatory lesions of the gastro-intestinal tract. Both onset of and relief from symptoms are abrupt. Diarrhoea is yellowish and forcibly expelled. Relief is obtained by movement while aggravation occurs after eating or drinking.

Condurango. Condor Plant.
The Ø is prepared from bark in tincture.

This plant produces a glucoside – condurangin which affects the nervous system causing an exaggerated gait. It can act constitutionally in promoting the general well-being of the patient. More specifically, there is an action on epithelial tissue causing hardening which may lead on to tumour formation. A guiding symptom is said to be cracks at the corners of the mouth. Chiefly used as a remedy to combat incipient cancerous states especially those in the abdomen.

Conium Maculatum. Hemlock. N.O. Umbelliferae.
The Ø is prepared from the fresh plant.

The alkaloid of this plant produces a paralytic action on nerve ganglia, especially the motor nerve endings. This leads to stiffness and a paralysis which tends to travel forward or upward. This remedy is of importance in treating paraplegic conditions and any weakness of hind limbs.

Convallaria Majalis. Lily of the Valley. N.O. Liliaceae.
The Ø is prepared from the fresh plant.

The active principle has the power to increase the quality of the heart's action and this determines its main use as a remedy in congestive heart conditions. It has little action on the heart muscle and is used mainly in valvular disease.

Copaiva. Balsam of Peru. N.O. Leguminosae.
The Ø is prepared from the balsam.

This substance produces a marked action on mucous membranes, especially those of the urinary and respiratory tracts causing a catarrhal inflammation. This action makes the remedy useful in the treatment of urethritis and cystitis. Pyelonephritis is one of the commoner conditions which could be helped.

Cortisone
The potentised steroid is used in practice to combat the effects of the over-prescribing of the crude substance where very often a single dose of the 200c potency will suffice along with clearing remedies such as *NUX VOMICA* and *THUJA*. In lower potency, e.g. 12c to 30c, it helps in certain skin conditions where dryness and redness predominate along with excessive itching.

Crataegus. Hawthorn. N.O. Rosaceae.
The Ø is prepared from the ripe fruit.

The active principle produces a fall in blood pressure and brings on dyspnoea. It acts on the heart muscle, causing an incease in the number and quality of contractions. The specific action on the heart muscle makes this a particularly useful remedy in the treatment of arrhythmic heart conditions.

Crotalus Horridus. Rattlesnake.
The Ø is prepared from trituration of the venom with lactose and subsequent dilution in glycerine.

This venom produces sepsis, haemorrhages and jaundice with decomposition of blood. The marked action of this poison on the vascular system makes it a valuable remedy in the treatment of many low-grade septic states with circulatory involvement, e.g. puerperal fever and wound infections. Septic conditions are accompanied by oozing of blood from any body orifice and are usually attended by jaundice. It should help in conditions such as adder-bite and clover poisoning.

Croton Tiglium. Croton Oil Seeds. N.O. Euphorbiaceae.
The Ø is prepared from the oil obtained from the seeds.

This oil produces violent diarrhoea and skin eruptions causing inflammation with a tendency to vesicle formation. This is one of the many useful remedies for controlling diarrhoea. This is usually accompanied by great urging, the stool being watery.

Cubeba Officinalis. Cubebs. N.O. Piperaceae.
The Ø is prepared from the dried unripe fruit.

The active principle acts on mucous membranes producing a catarrhal inflammation. Those of the uro-genital tract are particularly affected, the urine becoming cloudy and albuminous.

Cuprum Metallicum. Metallic Copper.
The Ø is prepared from trituration of the metal.

The symptoms produced by this metal are characterised by violence including paroxysms of cramping pains which follow no particular pattern. Muscles become contracted and show twitchings. In the central nervous system fits and convulsions occur and may take an epileptiform nature. The head is drawn to one side.

Curare. Woorari. Arrow Poison.
The Ø is prepared from dilutions in alcohol.

This poison produces muscular paralysis without impairing sensation or consciousness. Reflex action is diminished and a state of motor paralysis sets in. It decreases the output of adrenaline and brings about a state of nervous debility.

Damiana
The active principle of this plant has an affinity for the sexual system and is used mainly to promote libido in the male animal where sexual drive is weak. The action and results are variable but it is a remedy to keep in mind in this connection.

Digitalis Purpurea. Foxglove. N.O. Scrophulariaceae.
The Ø is prepared from the leaves.

The active principle of the foxglove causes marked slowness of the heart's action, the pulse being weak and irregular. This is a commonly-used remedy in heart conditions, helping to regulate the beat and producing a stable pulse. By increasing the output of the heart when used in low potencies it aids valvular function. This in turn increases the output of urine and helps reduce oedema.

Drosera Rotundifolia. Sundew. N.O. Droseraceae.
The Ø is prepared from the fresh plant.

The lymphatic and pleural systems together with synovial membranes are all affected by this plant. The laryngeal area is also subject to inflammatory processes, any stimulus producing a hypersensitive reaction.

Dulcamara. Woody Nightshade. N.O. Solanaceae.
The Ø is prepared from the green stems and leaves before flowering.

This plant belongs to the same family as *BELLADONNA, HYOSCYAMUS* and *STRAMONIUM*. Tissue affinities are with mucous membranes, glands and kidneys, producing inflammatory changes and interstitial haemorrhages. This remedy may benefit those conditions which arise as a result of exposure to wet and cold, especially when damp evenings follow a warm day. Such conditions commonly occur in autumn and diarrhoea occurring then may benefit. It has proved useful in the treatment of ringworm and could have a beneficial action on large fleshy warts.

Echinacea Angustifolia. Rudbeckia. N.O. Compositae.
The Ø is prepared from the whole plant.

Acute toxaemias with septic involvement of various tissues come within the sphere of action of this plant. It is a valuable remedy in the treatment of post-partum puerperal conditions where sepsis is evident. Generalised septic states having their origin in infected bites or stings will also benefit. This remedy acts best in low decimal potencies.

E. coli
This organism is found in the bowel and plays an essential role in the digestive process. As a remedy the nosode is used in bowel conditions where scouring develops after stress in the young animal or where the balance of the bowel flora has been interfered with.

Eel Serum.
The Ø is prepared from dried serum or solution in distilled water.

The serum of the eel produces an action on the blood equivalent to toxaemia. It affects the kidney particularly with secondary effects on the liver. Renal deposits are found in the urine along with haemoglobin. Threatened anaemic states develop. The cardiac system is also affected, sudden fainting spells being common.

Epigea Repens. Trailing Arbutus. N.O. Ericaceae.
The Ø is prepared from tincture of fresh leaves.

The main action of this remedy is on the urinary system where it produces a state of strangury with the production of renal calculi. It should be remembered in this connection as a useful remedy in cystitis of both male and female dogs and in the treatment of urethral and bladder stones.

Euphrasia Officinalis. Eyebright. N.O. Scrophulariaceae.
The Ø is prepared from the whole plant.

The active principle acts mainly on the conjunctival mucous membrane producing lachrymation. The cornea is also affected, opacities being common. This is one of the most useful remedies in the treatment of a variety of eye conditions, principally conjunctivitis and corneal ulcerations. Internal treatment should be supplemented by its use externally as a lotion diluted 1/10.

Ferrum Iodatum. Iodide of Iron.
Potencies are prepared from trituration of crystals subsequently dissolved in alcohol.

This salt is chiefly of interest as a remedy for iron deficiency associated with respiratory distress, mucous discharges containing blood being present. Metallic iron (*FERRUM METALLICUM*) and chloride of iron (*FERRUM MURIATICUM*) are also used in the treatment of iron deficiency, the former particularly for younger animals and the latter more indicated when heart symptoms such as a weak thready pulse are present.

Ferrum Phosphoricum. Ferric Phosphate.
Potencies are prepared from a solution in distilled water.

Febrile conditions in general are associated with this salt. It is frequently used in the early stages of inflammatory conditions which develop less rapidly than those calling for *ACONITUM*. Throat involvement is often the key to its selection. Pulmonary congestions may call for its use if haemorrhages are also present.

Ficus Religiosa. Pakur. N.O. Moraceae.
The Ø is prepared from fresh leaves in alcohol.

Haemorrhages of various kinds are associated with the toxic effects of this plant. Any condition which produces bleeding of a bright red character may indicate the need for this remedy. It could be of value in Coccidiosis, but generally respiratory rather than digestive upsets determine its use.

Fluoricum Acidum. Hydrofluoric Acid.
Potencies are prepared by distilling calcium fluoride with sulphuric acid.

It has an action on most tissues producing deep-seated ulcers and lesions of a destructive nature. It has been used successfully in the treatment of Actinomycosis and in ulcerative conditions of the mouth and throat. Any necrotic condition of bone is likely to benefit.

Folliculinum.
This is one of the ovarian hormones which has a beneficial action on the skin. Used mainly in practice in cases of miliary eczema and alopecia of both sexes. It can also be used in the treatment of eczemas of non-hormonal origin where the typical purply rashes predominate.

Formica. Formic Acid. The Ant. N.O. Hymenoptera.
The Ø is made from live ants.
This acid produces rheumatic-like pains along with deposits in the small joints. Occasionally in severe cases the spinal cord may be affected, giving rise to a state of temporary paralysis. It is chiefly used in veterinary practice as an anti-arthritis remedy especially affecting carpal and tarsal areas.

Gaertner-Bach.
Marked emaciation or malnutrition is associated with this nosode. Chronic gastro-enteritis occurs and there is a tendency for the animal to become infested with worms. There is an inability to digest fat. Chiefly used in the young animal showing malnutrition associated with other digestive problems.

Gelsemium Sempervirens. Yellow Jasmine. N.O. Loganiaceae.
The Ø is prepared from the bark of the root.
The affinity of this plant is with the nervous system, producing varying degrees of motor paralysis. This remedy has proved helpful as a supportive measure in hypomagnesaemia, aiding restoration of normal movement. Single paralysis of different nerves, e.g. the radial, may also benefit. Conditions which call for its use are usually attended by weakness and muscle tremors.

Glonoinum. Nitro-Glycerine.
Potencies are prepared from dilutions in alcohol.
This substance has an affinity with the brain and circulatory system causing sudden and violent convulsions and also congestion in the arterial system leading to throbbing and pulsations, seen in superficial vessels. It will be found of use in brain conditions arising from over-exposure to heat or the effects of the sun. It may also help the convulsions associated with hypomagnesaemia and allied conditions.

Graphites. Black Lead.
Potencies are prepared from triturations dissolved in alcohol.

This form of carbon has an affinity with skin and claws. Eruptions are common and its action on connective tissue tends to produce fibrotic conditions associated with malnutrition. Loss of hair occurs while purply moist eruptions ooze a sticky discharge. Abrasions develop into ulcers which may suppurate. Favourable sites for eczema are in the bends of joints and behind the ears.

Hamamelis Virginica. Witch Hazel. N.O. Hamamelidaceae.
The Ø is prepared from fresh bark of twigs and roots.

This plant has an affinity with the venous circulation, producing congestions and haemorrhages. The action on the veins is one of relaxation, with consequent engorgement. Any condition showing venous engorgement or congestion with passive haemorrhage should show improvement from the use of this remedy.

Hecla Lava. Hecla.
Potencies are prepared from trituration of the volcanic ash. Present in this ash are the substances which accompany lava formation, viz. Alumina, Lime and Silica.

Lymphoid tissue and the skeleton are areas which show the greatest affinity for this substance. The remedy is useful in the treatment of exostoses or tumours of the facial bones and in caries arising from dental disease. It has proved successful in the treatment of Actinomycosis affecting the maxillary and mandibular bones. It should help in the treatment of bony tumours generally.

Helleborus Niger. Christmas Rose. N.O. Ranunculaceae.
The Ø is produced from the juice of the fresh root.

The affinity of this plant is with the central nervous system and the alimentary canal. To a lesser extent the kidneys are involved. Vertigo-like movements arise together with convulsions. Vomiting and purging take place, stools being dysenteric. Heart action is slowed.

Hepar Sulphuris Calcareum. Impure Calcium Sulphide.
This substance is prepared by burning crude calcium carbonate with flowers of sulphur. Potencies are then prepared from the triturated ash.

This remedy is associated with suppurative processes, producing conditions which are extremely sensitive to touch. It causes catarrhal and purulent inflammation of the mucous membranes of the respiratory and alimentary tracts with involvement of the skin and lymphatic system. This remedy has a wide range of action and should be considered in any suppurative process showing extreme sensitivity to touch indicating acute pain. Low potencies of this remedy promote suppuration while high potencies — 200c and upwards — may abort the purulent process and promote resolution.

Hippozaeninum.
This nosode has been known for a long time having been made from glanders, a notifiable equine disease no longer encountered in Britain.

It has a wide range of use in many catarrhal conditions which are characterised by glutinous or honey-coloured discharges, e.g. sinusitis and ozaena with or without ulceration of nasal cartilages. It could be of great benefit in some forms of chronic viral rhinitis.

Hydrangea Arborescons. N.O. Hydrangeaceae.
The Ø is prepared from fresh leaves and young shoots.

This plant exerts a strong influence on the urinary system, especially on the bladder where it helps dissolve gravel. The prostate gland also comes within its range of action.

Hydrastis Canadensis. Golden Seal. N.O. Ranunculaceae.
The Ø is prepared from the fresh root.

Mucous membranes are affected by this plant, a catarrhal inflammation being established. Secretions generally are thick and yellow. Any catarrhal condition resulting in a muco-purulent discharge will come within the scope of this remedy, e.g. mild forms of metritis or sinusitis.

Hydrocotyle Asiatica. Indian Pennywort. N.O. Umbelliferae.
The Ø is prepared from the whole plant.

The main difficulty of this plant is with the skin and female genital system. It also has a lesser effect on the action of the liver. Skin conditions showing thickening of epidermis and roughening come within its sphere of action.

Hyoscyamus Niger. Henbane. N.O. Solanaceae.
The Ø is prepared from the fresh plant.

The active principle disturbs the central nervous system, producing symptoms of brain excitement and mania. Conditions which call for its use are not accompanied by inflammation (cf. *BELLADONNA*).

Hypericum Perforatum. N.O. Hyperiaceae.
The Ø is prepared from the whole fresh plant.

The active principle is capable of causing sensitivity to light on some skins in the absence of melanin pigment. The main affinity is with the nervous system causing hypersensitivity. Sloughing and necrosis of the skin may take place. This remedy is of prime importance in the treatment of lacerated wounds where nerve endings are damaged. In spinal injuries, especially of the coccygeal area, it gives good results. The specific action on nerves suggests its use in tetanus where, given early after injury, it helps prevent the spread of toxin. It can be used externally for lacerated wounds along with *CALENDULA*, both in a strength of 1/10. It has been found useful in the treatment of photosensitisation and similar allergies.

Iodium. Iodine. The Element.
Potencies are prepared from the tincture prepared by dissolving the element in alcohol. A 1% tincture is the strength used in preparation.

In large doses — iodism — sinuses and eyes are at first involved, leading to conjunctivitis and bronchitis. Iodine has a special affinity with the thyroid gland. Weakness and atrophy of muscles may follow excessive intake. The skin becomes dry and withered-looking and the appetite becomes voracious. Conditions which show a characteristic oppositeness of symptoms, e.g. tissue hyperplasia or atrophy, may need this remedy. It may be of use in ovarian dysfunction when the ovaries appear small and shrunken on rectal examination. It is a useful gland remedy and its specific relation to the thyroid should not be forgotten.

Ipecacuanha. N.O. Rubiaceae.
The Ø is prepared from the dried root. Emetine, an alkaloid, is its principal constituent.

This plant is associated with haemorrhages and has found a use in the treatment of post-partum bleeding where the blood comes in gushes.

Iris Versicolor. Blue Flag. N.O. Iridaceae.
The Ø is prepared from the fresh root.

This plant produces an action on various glands, principally the salivary, intestinal pancreas and thyroid. It has a reputation also for aiding the secretion of bile. Due to its action on the thyroid gland, swelling of the throat may occur. The remedy is chiefly used in veterinary practice in the treatment of disorders of the pancreas where it has given consistently good results.

Kali Arsenicum. Fowler's Solution. Potassium Arsenite.
Dilutions of this salt provide the Ø.

The main action which concerns us is exerted on the skin, a dry scaly eczema with itching being established. It is a good general skin remedy.

Kali Bichromicum. Potassium Bichromate.
Potencies are prepared from a solution in distilled water.

This salt acts on the mucous membranes of the stomach, intestines and respiratory tract with lesser involvement of other organs. Feverish states are absent. The action on the mucous membranes produces a catarrhal discharge of a tough stringy character with a yellow colour. This particular type of discharge is a strong guiding symptom for its use. It could be used in broncho-pneumonia, sinusitis and pylonephritis.

Kali Carbonicum. Potassium Carbonate.
Potencies are prepared from a solution in distilled water.

This salt is found in all plants and in the soil, the colloid material of cells containing potassium.

It produces a generalised weakness which is common to other potassium salts. Feverish states are absent. It could be a useful convalescent remedy.

Kali Chloricum. Potassium Chlorate.
Potencies are prepared from a solution in distilled water.

The urinary organs are chiefly affected, producing a blood-stained and albuminous urine with a high phosphate content.

Kali Hydriodicum. Potassium Iodide.
Potencies are prepared from triturations dissolved in alcohol.

This important drug produces an acrid watery discharge from the eyes and also acts on fibrous and connective tissue. Glandular swellings also appear. This is a widely used remedy in various conditions showing the typical eye and respiratory symptoms.

Kreosotum. Beechwood Kreosote.
The Ø is prepared from solution in rectified spirit.

This substance produces haemorrhages from small wounds with burning discharges and ulcerations. It also causes rapid decomposition of body fluids. Blepharitis occurs with a tendency to gangrene of the skin, while in the female dark blood appears from the uterus. This substance has been successfully used in threatened gangrenous states showing the typical early stages of spongy bleeding and ulceration.

Lachesis. Bushmaster. Surucucu Snake.
Trituration of venom dissolved in alcohol is the source of the solution which yields the potencies.

This venom produces decomposition of blood rendering it more fluid. There is a strong tendency to haemorrhage and sepsis with profound prostration. This is a useful remedy for Adder bites, helping to prevent septic complications and reducing swelling. It is particularly valuable if the throat develops inflammation causing left-sided swelling which may involve the parotid gland. Where haemorrhage takes place the blood is dark and does not clot readily while the skin surrounding any lesion assumes a purplish appearance.

Lathyrus Sativus. Chick Pea. N.O. Leguminosae.
The Ø is prepared from the flower and the pods.

This plant affects the anterior columns of the spinal cord, producing paralysis of the lower extremities. Nerve power generally is weakened. It should be considered in recumbent conditions associated with mineral deficiencies and in any state involving nerve weakness leading to local paralysis.

Ledum Palustre. Marsh Tea. Wild Rosemary. N.O. Ericaceae.
The Ø is prepared from the whole plant.

The active principle produces tetanus-like symptoms with twitching of muscles. It is one of the main remedies for punctured wounds, especially when the surrounding area becomes cold and discoloured. Insect bites respond well. Also injuries to the eye.

Lemna Minor. Duckweed. N.O. Lemnaceae.
The Ø is prepared from whole fresh plants.

This is a remedy for catarrhal conditions affecting mainly the nasal passages; a muco-purulent nasal discharge develops which is extremely offensive. In the alimentary sphere diarrhoea and flatulence can occur.

Lilium Tigrinum. Tiger Lily. N.O. Liliaceae.
The Ø is prepared from fresh leaves and flowers.

The action is mainly on the pelvic organs, producing conditions which arise from uterine or ovarian disturbances. Urine is scanty and frequently passed. An irregular pulse accompanies an increased heart rate. Congestion and blood-stained discharges arise from the uterus and there may be slight prolapse. Indicated in some forms of pyometra where blood is present and also in ovarian disturbances.

Lithium Carbonicum. Lithium Carbonate.
The Ø is prepared from trituration of the dried salt.

This salt produces a chronic arthritic state with a uric acid diathesis. There is difficulty in passing urine, which contains mucus and a red sandy deposit. Cystitis develops leading to a dark urine. It is a useful remedy to consider in some forms of arthritis and urinary conditions producing uric acid deposits.

Lobelia Inflata. Indian Tobacco. N.O. Lobeliaceae.
The Ø is prepared from the dried leaves with subsequent dilution in alcohol.

The active principle acts as a vaso-motor stimulant impeding respiration and producing symptoms of inappetance and relaxation of muscles. It is of value in emphysematous conditions and as a general convalescent remedy.

Lycopodium Clavatum. Club Moss. N.O. Lycopodiaceae.
The Ø is prepared from trituration of the spores and dilution in alcohol. The spores are inactive until triturated and potentised.

The active principle acts chiefly on the digestive and renal systems.

The respiratory system is also affected, pneumonia being a frequent complication. There is general lack of gastric function and very little food will satisfy. The abdomen becomes bloated with tenderness over the liver. The glycogenic function of the liver is interfered with. This is a very useful remedy in various digestive, urinary and respiratory conditions, a guiding symptom being that complaints frequently show an aggravation in the late afternoon or early evening. It is the first remedy of choice in the digestive form of acetonaemia while its action on the skin suggests its use in alopecia.

Lycopus Virginicus. Bugle Weed. N.O. Labiatae.
The Ø is prepared from fresh whole plant.

The active principle of this plant reduces blood pressure and causes passive haemorrhages. The main sphere of action which concerns veterinary practice is on the cardiac system where the pulse becomes weak and irregular. The heart's action is increased and is accompanied by difficult breathing and cyanosis. Breathing assumes a wheezy character and may produce a blood-tinged cough.

Magnesia Phosphorica. Phosphate of Magnesium.
Potencies are prepared from trituration of the salt in solution.

This salt acts on muscles, producing a cramping effect with spasm. It is a valuable remedy to be remembered as supportive treatment in hypomagnesaemia where its prompt use will limit the tendency to brain damage and help fix the element in the system, as otherwise it may be quickly excreted.

Malandrinum.
This nosode has been developed from the condition known as grease in the horse after trituration of affected material and discharge.

It is used mainly in the treatment of chronic skin eruptions and discharges. In this connection it is worth remembering as a remedy which might help some forms of ear canker.

Melilotus. Sweet Clover. N.O. Leguminosae.
The Ø is prepared from the whole fresh plant.

This plant is associated with profuse haemorrhages. Clover contains a haemolytic agent which prevents clotting of blood after mechanical injuries. It should be remembered as a possibly useful remedy in haematomas and subcutaneous bleeding of unknown origin.

Mercurius. Mercurius Solubilis. Mercury.
Potencies are prepared from triturations and dilutions in alcohol.

This metal affects most organs and tissues, producing cellular degeneration with consequent anaemia. Salivation accompanies most complaints and gums become spongy and bleed easily. Diarrhoea is common, stools being slimy and blood-stained. Conditions calling for its use are worse in the period from sunset to sunrise.

Mercurius Corrosivus. Mercuric Chloride. Corrosive Sublimate.
Potencies are prepared from triturations and subsequent dilution.

This salt has a somewhat similar action to *MERC SOL.*, but generally the symptoms produced are more severe. It produces severe tenesmus of the lower bowel leading to dysentery and also has a destructive action on kidney tissue. Discharges from mucous surfaces assume a greenish tinge. It could be of value in severe cases of coccidiosis.

Mercurius Cyanatus. Cyanate of Mercury.
Potencies are prepared from triturations and dilutions.

This particular salt produces an action similar to that associated with bacterial toxins. A haemorrhagic tendency with prostration is a common feature. Ulceration of the mucous membranes of the mouth and throat commonly occur. A greyish membrane surrounds these ulcerated surfaces. The phyaryngeal area is one of the main regions to be affected, redness of the membrane preceding necrosis in the later stages.

Mercurius Dulcis. Calomel. Mercurous Chloride.
Potencies are prepared from triturations and dilution.

This salt has an affinity with the ear and liver especially. Hepatitis with jaundice may result. It is worth considering as a possibly useful remedy in mild forms of cirrhosis.

Mercurius Iodatus Flavus. Yellow Iodide of Mercury.
Potencies are prepared from triturations in dilution.

Mercurous Iodide produces a tendency to glandular induration with attendant coating of the tongue. Sub-maxillary and parotid glands become swollen, more pronounced on the right side. Various swellings of glandular tissue come within the sphere of this remedy, e.g. parotitis and lymphadenitis generally. It could be of value in actinobacillosis when lesions attack on the right side.

Mercurius Iodatus Ruber. Red Iodide of Mercury.
Potencies are prepared from trituration of the salt.

Mercuric Iodide also has a tendency to produce glandular swellings, but in this case the left side of the throat is involved. Stiffness of neck mucles may be a prominent symptom.

Millefolium. Yarrow. N.O. Compositae.
The Ø is prepared from the whole plant.

Haemorrhages occur from various parts from the action of this plant. The blood is bright red.

Mineral Extract.
This substance has recently been researched and has been shown to have a beneficial effect on certain forms of joint trouble, e.g. arthritis and stiffness especially of the carpal and tarsal areas.

Mixed Grasses.
Some animals show an allergic response to grasses in early spring and summer when excessive itching and skin lesions develop. A combination of various grasses in potency appear to help these conditions and can be combined with other selected remedies.

Morgan-Bach.
Clinical observation has revealed the symptom picture of the bacillus Morgan to cover in general digestive and respiratory conditions. It has a secondary action on fibrous tissues and skin and is mainly used in practice to treat inflammatory conditions, especially acute eczema, combined with appropriate remedies.

Murex Purpurea. Purple Fish.
The Ø is prepared from the dried secretion of the purple gland of one of the Murex species.

It exerts its action mainly on the female genital system producing irregularities of the oestrus cycle. It has been employed both in anoestrus and for stimulating ovulation, but probably it will give best results in cystic ovary leading to nymphomania.

Muriaticum Acidum. Hydrochloric Acid.
Potencies are prepared from dilutions, in distilled water.

This acid produces a blood condition analogous to that associated with septic feverish states of a chronic nature. There is a tendency for ulcers to form. The throat becomes dark red and oedematous while ulceration of the lips accompanies swollen gums and neck glands.

Naja Tripudians. Cobra.
Potencies are prepared from trituration of the venom and subsequent dilution in alcohol. Alternatively the Ø may be prepared by dilution of the pure venom.

This poison produces a bulbar paralysis. Haemorrhages are scanty but oedema is marked. The underlying tissues appear dark purple after a bite, blood-stained fluid being present in large quantities. Loss of limb control supervenes. The heart is markedly affected. It could be of use in angio-neurotic oedema.

Natrum Muriaticum. Common Salt. Sodium Chloride.
Potencies are prepared from triturations dissolved in distilled water.

Excessive intake of common salt leads to anaemia, evidenced by dropsy or oedema of various parts. White blood cells are increased while mucous membranes are rendered dry. This is a remedy which is of value in unthrifty conditions arising as a result of anaemia or chronic nephritis.

Natrum Sulphuricum. Sodium Sulphate.
The Ø is prepared from trituration of the salt.

Glauber's Salt (as it is commonly called) produces a state of weakness where the animal has been exposed to damp. The liver is affected and there is a tendency to wart formation. Hepatitis sometimes occurs with jaundice. Flatulent distension and watery diarrhoea supervene. Experience has shown that this remedy has proved to be of great value where there has been a history of head injury leading to a variety of seemingly unrelated conditions.

Nitricum Acidum. Nitric Acid.
Potencies are prepared from a solution in distilled water.

This acid particularly affects body outlets where skin and mucous membranes meet. It produces ulceration and blisters in the mouth and causes offensive discharges. The ulceration may also affect mucous membranes elsewhere and it has been of benefit in some forms of mucosal disease.

Nux Vomica. Poison Nut. N.O. Loganiaeceae.
The Ø is prepared from the seeds.

Digestive disturbances and congestions are associated with this plant, flatulence and indigestion being commonly encountered. Stools are generally hard.

Ocimum Canum. Brazilian Alfavaca. N.O. Labiatae.
The Ø is prepared from the fresh leaves.

This remedy exerts its action mainly on the urinary system, producing a turbid urine of a deep yellow colour. The urine itself is slimy and purulent with a musky sweet smell. Mainly used in urinary disturbances showing the typical symptoms.

Opium. Poppy. N.O. Papaveraceae.
The Ø is prepared from the powder after trituration.

Opium produces an insensibility of the nervous system with stupor and torpor. There is a lack of vital reaction. All complaints are characterised by soporific states. Pupils are contracted and the eyes assume a staring look.

Ovarium.
This is also one of the ovarian hormones in potency. It covers a range of action similar to *FOLLICULINUM* but the results have been shown to be less satisfactory than with the latter remedy.

Palladium. The Metal.
Potencies are prepared from triturations and subsequent dilution in alcohol.

This element produces its main action on the female genital system, especially the ovaries causing an inflammation with a tendency to pelvic peritonitis. The right ovary is more usually affected. Pelvic disorders arising as a result of ovaritis should also benefit.

Pancreas — Pancreatinum.
The Ø is prepared from pancreas extract after trituration.

It is used on various disorders of the pancreas either on its own or combined with selected remedies to suit the individual case. In pancreatitis it can be used along with the digestive enzyme Trypsin.

Pareira. Velvet Leaf. N.O. Menispermaceae.
The Ø is prepared from tincture of fresh root.

The active principle of this plant exerts its action mainly on the urinary system, producing catarrhal inflammation of the bladder with a tendency to calculus formation. In the female there may be vaginal or uterine discharge. It is a useful remedy to consider in cases of vesical calculus where the animal is presented with acute strangury and distress.

Parotidinum.
This is the nosode of mumps and in veterinary practice it is a useful remedy in the treatment of cases of parotid gland swellings and associated structures. It may be used either on its own or combined with indicated remedies.

Petroleum. Rock Spirit.
The Ø is prepared from the oil.

This substance produces cutaneous eruptions and catarrhal mucous membranes. Eczematous eruptions develop around ears and eyelids and feet, producing fissures which are slow to heal. The skin is usually dry. Complaints are usually worse in cold weather. A useful remedy for some forms of chronic skin conditions where symptoms agree.

Phosphoricum Acidum. Phosphoric Acid.
Potencies are prepared from a dilution of the acid in distilled water.

This acid produces a debilitating state in which flatulence and diarrhoea are common features.

Phosphorus. The Element.
The Ø is prepared from trituration of red phosphorus.

This important substance produces an inflammatory and degenerative effect on mucous membranes and causes bone destruction and necrosis of liver and other parenchymatous organs. It has a profound effect on eye structures especially the retina and iris. There is a marked haemorrhagic diathesis associated with this remedy, and small haemorrhages appear on the skin and mucous membranes. Its uses in practice are wide and varied and it is one of the most important remedies in the pharmacopoeia.

Phytolacca Decandra. Pore Root. N.O. Phytolaccaceae.
The Ø is prepared from the whole fresh plant.

A state of restlessness and prostration is associated with this plant, together with glandular swellings. It is chiefly used in veterinary practice to combat swellings of the mammary glands in particular when the glands become hard and painful. Abscesses may develop together with mastitis of varying degree. In the male, testicular swelling may occur. The remedy is of immense value in mastitis and other forms of mammary swellings.

Platina. The Metal Platinum.
The Ø is prepared from trituration of the metal with lactose.

This metal has a specific action on the female genital system, especially the ovaries where inflammation readily develops. Cystic ovaries develop frequently.

Plumbum Metallicum. The Metal Lead.
The Ø is prepared from trituration with sugar of milk.

A state of paralysis preceded by pain is produced by exposure to or ingestion of lead. It affects the central nervous system and also causes liver damage leading to jaundiced states. Blood pictures show anaemia. Paralyses of lower limbs develop and convulsions are common, leading to coma. It should be remembered as a useful remedy to consider in degenerative renal states associated with liver involvement.

Podophyllum. May Apple. N.O. Ranuculaceae.
The Ø is prepared from the whole fresh plants.

The active principle of this plant exerts its action mainly on the duodenum and small intestine causing an enteritis. The liver and rectum are also affected. Distension of the abdomen occurs with a tendency to lie on the abdomen. Colicky pains develop with tenderness over the liver. A watery greenish diarrhoea may alternate with constipation. It is a useful remedy for gastro-intestinal disorders of young animals especially and for liver and perital congestion.

Pseudomonas.
This is the potentised organism used in the treatment of cases of Pseudomonas infection. It can be combined with selected remedies in this event.

Psorinum. Scabies Vesicle.
The Ø is prepared from trituration of the dried vesicle.

This nosode produces a state of debility, especially after acute illness with skin symptoms predominating. All discharges are unpleasant. Chronic ophthalmia is occasionally seen along with otitis media and externa producing an offensive brownish discharge. Skin conditions are accompanied by severe itching. Animals needing this remedy prefer warmth.

Ptelea. Water Ash. N.O. Rutaceae.
The Ø is prepared from the bark or root.

This plant produces its main action on the stomach and liver. Hepatitis occurs with tenderness over the liver and stomach areas. This is a good 'cleansing' remedy in that it will aid elimination of toxins and thereby help clear conditions such as eczema and asthmatic tendencies.

Pulsatilla. Anemone. N.O. Ranunculaceae.
The Ø is prepared from the entire plant when in flower.

Mucous membranes come within the sphere of action of this plant, thick muco-purulent discharges being produced. It has proved useful in the treatment of ovarian hypofunction and in retained placenta.

Pyrogenium. Artificial Sepsin.
The Ø is prepared from solutions of raw protein in distilled water.

This nosode has a specific relation to septic inflammations associated with offensive discharges. It is indicated in all septic conditions where the animal presents a clinical picture of raised temperature alternating with a weak thready pulse, or vice versa. It should be used in potencies of 200c and upwards.

Ranunculus Bulbosus. Buttercup. N.O. Ranunculaceae.
The Ø is prepared from the whole plant.

The action is mainly on muscular tissue and skin, producing a hypersensitivity to touch. Skin lesions take the form of papular and vesicular eruptions which may cluster together into oval-shaped groups.

Rescue Remedy.
This is one of the many Bach Flower remedies and possibly the one most widely known and used. These remedies are not potentised like homoeopathic remedies but have been shown in practice to exert remarkable curative properties. Rescue Remedy is used to benefit the patient after exposure to any traumatic experience e.g. stress, shock and post-operative trauma. A very useful remedy to revive weak puppies after birth.

Rhododendron. Snow Rose. N.O. Ericaceae.
The Ø is prepared from the fresh leaves.

This shrub is associated with muscular and joint stiffness. Orchitis is not uncommon, with the testicles becoming hard and indurated.

Rhus Toxicodendron. Poison Oak. N.O. Anacardiaceae.
The Ø is prepared from the fresh leaves.

The active principles of this tree affect skin and muscles together with mucous membranes and fibrous tissues producing tearing pains and blistery eruptions. Symptoms of stiffness are relieved by movement. Involvement of the skin leads to a reddish rash with vesicles and produces a cellulitis of neighbouring tissues. It could be a useful remedy in muscle and joint conditions which show a characteristic improvement on exercise.

Rumex Crispus. Yellow Dock. N.O. Polygonaceae.
The Ø is prepared from the fresh root.

The active principle of this plant causes a diminution in the secretions from mucous membranes. Chronic gastritis occurs accompanied by an aversion to food and a watery diarrhoea. Mucous discharges take place from the trachea and nose. These tend to assume a frothy appearance. It is a useful remedy in some forms of respiratory affections.

Ruta Graveolens. Rue. N.O. Rutaceae.
The Ø is prepared from the whole fresh plant.

Ruta produces its action on the periosteum and cartilages with a secondary effect on the eyes and uterus. Deposits form particularly around the carpal joints. It also has a selective action on the lower bowel and rectum and could prove useful in mild forms of rectal prolapse. It has been known to facilitate labour by increasing the tone of uterine contractions.

Sabina. Savine. N.O. Coniferae.
The Ø is prepared from the oil dissolved in alcohol.

The uterus is the main seat of action producing a tendency to abortion. There is also an action on fibrous tissues and serous membranes. It is associated with haemorrhages of bright red blood which remains fluid. This remedy has its main use in uterine conditions including retained placenta. Persistent post-partum bleeding may also be arrested.

Sanguinaria. Blood Root. N.O. Papaveraceae.
The Ø is prepared from the fresh root.

An alkaloid — sanguinarine — contained in this plant has an affinity with the circulatory system leading to congestion and redness of skin. The female genital system is affected, inflammation of ovaries occurring. Small cutaneous haemorrhages arise in various sites. Stiffness of fore-legs, especially the left shoulder region may be seen.

Secale Cornutum. Ergot of Rye. N.O. Fungi.
The Ø is prepared from the fresh fungus.

Ergot produces marked contraction of smooth muscle, causing a diminution of blood supply to various areas. This is particularly seen in peripheral blood vessels, especially of the feet. Stools are dark green alternating with dysentery. Bleeding of dark blood occurs from the uterus with putrid discharges. The skin becomes dry and shrivelled-looking with a tendency for gangrene to form. Because of its circulatory action and its effect on smooth muscle, it is useful in some uterine conditions, e.g. post-partum bleeding of dark blood, and in any condition with impairment of peripheral circulation.

Sepia Officinalis. Cuttlefish.
Potencies are prepared from trituration of the dried liquid from the ink bag.

Portal congestion and stasis are associated with this substance, along with disturbances of function in the female genital system. Prolapse of the uterus may occur or a tendency thereto. It will regulate the entire oestrus cycle and should always be given as a routine preliminary remedy in treatment. It also has an action on the skin and has given good results in the treatment of ringworm. Post-partum discharges of various sorts will usually respond. It is also capable of encouraging the natural maternal instinct in those animals which are indifferent or hostile to their offspring.

Silicea. Pure Flint.
Potencies are prepared from triturations dissolved in alcohol.

The main action of this substance is on bone, where it is capable of causing caries and necrosis. It also causes abscesses and fistulae of connective tissue with secondary fibrous growths. There is a tendency for all wounds to suppurate. This is a widely-used remedy indicated in many suppurative processes of a chronic nature.

Solidago Virga. Golden Rod. N.O. Compositae.
The Ø is prepared from the whole fresh plant.

This plant produces an inflammatory action on parenchymatous organs, particularly the kidney. The urine is scanty, reddish and accompanied by albumen deposits. Prostatic enlargement is frequently encountered. It is a useful remedy to consider in certain cases of renal insufficiency either with or without prostatic enlargement in the male animal.

Spigelia. Pink Root. N.O. Loganiaceae.
The Ø is prepared from the dried herb.

This plant has an affinity for the nervous system and also exerts an action on the cardiac region and the eye, producing ophthalmia and dilated pupils. A useful remedy for certain eye conditions especially if pain above the eyes can be elicited from the patient.

Spongia Tosta. Roasted Sponge.
Potencies are prepared from dilutions in alcohol.

This substance produces symptoms related to the respiratory and cardiac spheres. The lymphatic system is also affected. The thyroid gland becomes enlarged. The general action on glands suggests its use in lymphadenitis. It is principally used as a heart remedy after respiratory infections.

Squilla Maritima. Sea Onion. N.O. Liliaceae.
The Ø is prepared from the dried bulb.

This substance acts especially on the mucous membranes of the respiratory tract. The digestive and renal systems are also affected. Nasal discharges develop accompanied by a dry cough which later becomes mucoid. There is an urging to urinate, the urine being watery and profuse. It is a useful remedy for heart and kidney affections being especially valuable in dropsical conditions.

Staphisagria. Stavesacre. N.O. Ranunculaceae.
The Ø is prepared from the seeds.

The nervous system is mainly involved with this plant but there is also an action on the genito-urinary tract and the skin. A useful remedy in cystitis, but probably its most important indication is as a post-operative remedy where it acts on the mental level reducing psychological trauma and hastening the healing of wounds. It is also of benefit in the treatment of hormonal eczemas and alopecias.

Stramonium. Thorn Apple. N.O. Solanaceae.
The Ø is prepared from the whole fresh plant and fruit.

The active principle of this shrub produces its main action on the central nervous system, especially the cerebrum, producing a staggering gait with a tendency to fall forward on to the left side. Dilation of the pupils occurs with a fixed staring look. A useful remedy to consider in brain disturbances where overall symptoms agree.

Streptococcus and Staphylococcus.
Streptococcus nosode is used in conditions associated with infections by this organism, e.g. erythematous rashes, tonsillitis and nephritis with associated pyelitis. It can be combined with other selected

remedies. Staphylococcus Aurens is the main remedy to consider in staphylococcal affections, e.g. abscesses and mastitis. These nosodes are usually used in 30c potency.

Strophanthus. Onage. N.O. Apocynaceae.
The Ø is prepared from the seeds dissolved in alcohol.

This shrub produces an increase in the contractile power of striped muscle. It acts especially on the heart, increasing systole. The amount of urine passed is increased and albuminuria may be present. This is a useful heart remedy to help remove oedema. It is a safe and useful diuretic especially for the older animal.

Strychninum. Strychnine. Alkaloid Contained in Nux Vomica.
Potencies are prepared from solutions in distilled water.

This alkaloid stimulates the motor centres of the spinal cord and increases the depth of respirations. All reflexes are rendered more active and pupils become dilated. Rigidity of muscles occurs especially of the neck and back with jerking and twitching of limbs. Muscle tremors and tetanic convulsions set in rapidly. This remedy may prove useful in severe forms of hypomagnesaemia or cerebro-cortical necrosis if the specific symptoms are present.

Sulfonal. A derivative of Coal Tar.
The Ø is prepared from solution in alcohol or trituration with lactose.

This substance affects the central nervous system causing irregular movements, twitchings and inco-ordination of muscles which become stiff with a paralytic tendency. A useful remedy to consider in cases of cerebro-cortical affections showing the typical neuro-muscular symptoms.

Sulphur. The Element.
Potencies are prepared from trituration and subsequent dilution in alcohol.

This element has a wide range of action, but it is chiefly used in skin conditions such as mange and eczema and also as an inter-current remedy to aid the action of other remedies.

Symphytum. Comfrey. N.O. Boraginaceae.
The Ø is prepared from the fresh plant.

The root of this plant produces a substance which stimulates the growth of epithelium on ulcerated surfaces and hastens the union of bone in fractures. It should always be given as a routine remedy in fractures as an aid to healing. Together with other vulneraries like *ARNICA* it is indicated in the treatment of injuries in general. It is also a prominent eye remedy.

Syzygium. Jumbul. N.O. Myrtaceae.
The Ø is prepared from trituration of seeds and subsequent dilution in alcohol.

This plant exerts an action on the pancreas and this defines its use in practice, especially in diabetes where it reduces the specific gravity of the urine and reduces thirst and controls output of urine.

Tabacum. Tobacco.
This substance produces nausea and vomiting with intermittent pulse and weakness. In extreme cases there is a picture of muscular weakness and collapse.

Its main use in canine medicine would be in the treatment of sickness associated with movement, especially travel by sea.

Tarentula Hispanica. Spanish Spider.
The Ø is prepared from trituration of the whole insect.

Hysterical states are associated with this poison, and there is also a stimulatory action on the uro-genital system. A useful remedy to consider in cases of hysteria and epilepsy accompanied or preceded by excitement. Excessive libido (satyriasis) in the male may be helped.

Tellurium. The Metal.
The Ø is prepared from trituration with lactose.

This element exerts an influence on skin, eyes and ears. There is also an action on the sacral region. Cataracts and conjunctivitis develop. In the skin herpetic eruptions appear which assume an annular shape. This remedy is a useful one to consider in some forms of ear trouble where eruptions appear on the ear flap.

Terebinthinae. Oil of Turpentine.
Potencies are prepared from a solution in alcohol.

Haemorrhages are produced from various surfaces, urinary symptoms predominating. There is difficulty in urinating and blood commonly occurs in the urine. Bleeding may also take place in the uterus, especially after parturition. It is principally used in acute nephritis associated with haematuria and a sweet-smelling urine. This odour has been likened to that of violets.

Testosterone.
This is a male hormone secreted by the testicle and is used mainly in the treatment of miliary eczema and alopecia in the castrated male. It has been shown clinically to be less effective in this connection than the female hormones *FOLLICULINUM* and *OVARIUM*. It has also been used with varying success in the treatment of anal adenoma.

Thallium Acetas.
The metallic salt is triturated and dissolved in alcohol.

This metal exerts an action on the endocrine system and also on the skin and neuro-muscular system where it produces paralysis followed by muscular atrophy. The skin conditions frequently result in alopecia. It is used mainly in the treatment of trophic skin conditions, e.g. chronic alopecia and myelitis.

Thlaspi Bursa Pastoralis. Shepherd's Purse. N.O. Cruciferae.
The Ø is prepared from the fresh plant.

This plant produces haemorrhages with a uric acid diathesis. It favours expulsion of blood clots from the uterus and is indicated after miscarriage. There is frequency of urination, the urine being heavy and turbid with a reddish sediment. Cystitis is commonly seen with blood-stained urine.

Thuja Occidentalis. Arbor Vitae. N.O. Coniferae.
The Ø is prepared from fresh twigs.

Thuja produces a condition which favours the formation of warty growths and tumours. It acts mainly on the skin and uro-genital system. Warts and herpetic eruptions develop, the neck and abdomen being the favourite sites. This remedy is of great importance in the treatment of skin conditions accompanied by the development of warty growths which bleed easily. Papillomatous warts are especially influenced and this action may be enhanced by the external application of the remedy in Ø form.

Thyroidinum. Thyroid Gland.
Potencies are prepared from triturations and dilution in alcohol.

Anaemia, emaciation and muscular weakness are associated with excess of thyroid secretion. There is dilation of the pupils with prominence. Heart rate is increased. This remedy may be of use in the treatment of alopecia and allied skin conditions.

Trinitrotoluene. T.N.T.
Potencies are prepared from a solution in distilled water.

This substance exerts a destructive influence on red blood cells, causing haemolysis with consequent loss of haemoglobin. This produces anaemia and this is the principle of treatment by this remedy. It could be of use in babesiasis and similar conditions.

Tuberculinum Bovinum.
This nosode should be considered if a case of tuberculosis is encountered, but apart from this it is indicated in the treatment of osteomyelitis and some forms of peritonitis and pleurisy with effusions.

Uranium Nitricum. Uranium Nitrate.
The Ø is prepared from solution in distilled water.

Glycosuria and polyuria are the main objective symptoms associated with the provings of this salt. There is a marked action on the pancreas where it influences digestive function. Large amounts of urine are passed. This is a useful remedy in pancreatitis where it follows well after the remedy *IRIS VERSICOLOR*.

Urtica Urens. Stinging Nettle. N.O. Urticaceae.
The Ø is prepared from the fresh plant.

The nettle causes agalactia with a tendency to the formation of calculi. There is a general uric acid diathesis with urticarial swellings being present on the skin. There is diminished secretion of urine. The mammary glands become enlarged with surrounding oedema. This is a very useful remedy in various renal and skin conditions. In the treatment of uric acid tendencies it acts by thickening the urine which contains increased deposits of urates.

Ustilago Maydis. Corn Smut. N.O. Fungi.
The Ø is prepared from trituration of the fungus with lactose.

This substance has an affinity for the genital organs of both sexes, particularly the female where the uterus is markedly affected. Alopecia of varying degrees develops accompanying a dry coat. Uterine bleeding occurs, the blood being bright-red and partly clotted. Haemorrhages occur post-partum. In the male satyriasis occurs and this leads to one of its main uses in veterinary practice to control excessive sexual activity. The uterine action should not be overlooked.

Uva Ursi. Bearberry. N.O. Ericaceae.
The Ø is prepared from dried leaves and fruit.

The active principles are associated with disturbances of the urinary system. Cystitis commonly occurs and the urine may contain blood, pus and mucus. Kidney involvement is usually confined to the pelvis causing a purulent inflammation. This is one of the main remedies used in the treatment of cystitis and pyelonephritis.

Veratrum Album. White Hellebore. N.O. Liliaceae.
The Ø is prepared from root stocks.

A picture of collapse is presented by the action of this plant. Extremities become cold and signs of cyanosis appear. Purging occurs, the watery diarrhoea being accompanied by exhaustion. The body surface quickly becomes cold and the stools are greenish. Signs of abdominal pain precede the onset of diarrhoea.

Viburnum Opulus. Water Elder. Cranberry. N.O. Caprifoliaceae.
The Ø is prepared from the fresh bark.

Muscular cramps are associated with the action of this plant. The female genital system is markedly affected, chiefly the uterus, producing a tendency to abortion in the first quarter of pregnancy, sterility being a common sequel. It is principally used in the treatment of animals with a history of repeated miscarriages.

Vipera. Common Viper.
Potencies are prepared from diluted venom.

This poison causes paresis of the hind limbs with a tendency to paralysis. Symptoms extend upwards. Skin and subcutaneous tissues become swollen after a bite, with livid tongue and swollen lips developing. Disturbances of liver function produce a jaundice of the visible mucous membranes. Inflammation of the veins occurs with attendant oedema. Oedematous states arising from venous congestion provide conditions suitable for its use and it should be remembered as a possibly useful remedy in liver dysfunction.

Zincum Metallicum. Zinc. The Metal.
Potencies are prepared from trituration with subsequent dilution in alcohol.
  This element produces a state of anaemia with a decrease in the number of red cells. There is a tendency to fall towards the left side with weakness and trembling of muscles. It is a useful remedy in suppressed feverish states accompanied by anaemia and may prove useful in brain conditions showing typical symptoms.

Nosodes and Oral Vaccines

Reference to nosodes and oral vaccines has already been made in the preface to this book, and it is only necessary to add that all disease products are rendered innocuous after the third centesimal potency, which is equivalent to a strength or dilution of 1/1,000,000. They are used in the 30c potency.

Bacillinum.
This remedy is prepared from tuberculous material. It is extremely useful in the treatment of ringworm and similar skin diseases.

Carcinosin.
The Nosode of Carcinoma.
  This remedy can be helpful in cases of glandular enlargements accompanied by feverish states.

E. Coli Nosode and Oral Vaccine.
Prepared from various strains of E. Coli. It has been found in practice that the strain which has given the most consistent results is the one which was prepared originally from a human source. Both treatment and prevention of coli-bacillosis come within its range and also the specific form of mastitis associated with E. Coli infection.

Folliculinum.
The nosode prepared from the corpus luteum is used chiefly in the treatment of various ovarian and allied conditions.

Oopherinum.
This is the actual ovarian hormone. Ovarian troubles come within its sphere of action, e.g. sterility dependent on ovarian dysfunction. It has also been used in some forms of skin disorder thought to be associated with hormone imbalance.

Psorinum. Scabies Vesicle.
This is a valuable skin remedy. It should be kept in mind as a possibly useful addition to the more commonly used remedies. Ringworm may respond as well as other conditions attended by dry coat and great itching.

Pyrogenium. Pyrogen.
This nosode is prepared from decaying animal protein. Despite its origin it is an extremely valuable remedy in the treatment of septicaemic or toxaemic states where vital reserves are low. One of the main indications for its use is illness attended by a high temperature alternating with a weak thready pulse, or alternatively a low temperature with a firm pulse. All discharges and septic states are extremely offensive. It could have a vital part to play in puerperal feverish conditions, and has been used in retained afterbirth after abortions.

Salmonella Nosode and Oral Vaccine.
Prepared from the common Salmonella organisms associated with this disease and used both prophylactically and therapeutically.

Streptococcus Nosode and Oral Vaccine.
Prepared from strains of haemolytic streptococci. It is used in various infections associated with these bacteria.

Sycotic Co. One of the Bowel Nosodes.
This is one of a group of nosodes prepared from the non-lactose fermenting bacilli found in the large intestine. Each one is related to certain homoeopathic remedies and used mainly in conjunction with

them. They are also used by themselves. Sycotic Co. has been used successfully in intestinal conditions producing catarrhal inflammation on mucous membranes.

Tuberculinum Aviare.

Avian sources provide the material for this nosode. This nosode may prove useful in the treatment of some forms of pneumonia, along with indicated remedies. Chronic conditions are the most likely to benefit.

Index